90% Right CAN BE 100% Wrong

Applying Principles to Achieve Your Full Potential

Todd Bennett, PhD

90% Right Can Be 100% Wrong
Copyright © 2010 by Todd Bennett, PhD

Borderline Publishing LLC
305 N. Steelhead Way
Boise, ID 83704
www.borderlinepublishing.com

ISBN 978-0984504534 (Paperback)

Cover design by Tara Mayberry
Picture by Dakota Bennett Photography

Printed in the United States of America on post-consumer recycled paper

Borderline
Publishing

Table of Contents

Forward

Todd Bennett is my friend. I cherish the talks we have had and the too limited times we have enjoyed on the ski slope, the lunch table, and the fishing hole. Early on I discovered that Todd is different. He has the ability to clear away the smoke and fog from complex situations and bring the pristine clarity that the moment demands.

Our friendship began because I kept running into people who sought his counsel and found healing for their lives through living the principles he described. Soon I was sending everyone I could to Todd's office for help. His unwavering commitment to truth and the principled life has created an environment that brings wholeness to marriages in a day when couples hunger for insight and intimacy.

As you read Dr. Bennett's book, don't be surprised if you find tears of joy line your face from a new insight. Be warned that you may be challenged to go beyond your feelings to confront your fears. Like Ruben and Sarah in the early pages of the book, you will learn about treasures that reap immediate results but take a lifetime to unearth. You may read words that you wish you had not because they reveal something deep in your core that you know is needing character. This book is valuable for everyone who wants to grow and succeed.

I have been a teacher, a coach, and have now pastored a thriving church for more than two decades. In that time I have not known a more gifted counselor or entrusted my private conversations with such confidence. It is my prayer that this book will become to you a valuable friend. You will read it and want to revisit its pages again and again to be reminded of principles that bring freedom–principles Todd teaches will never change.

God Bless you as your read these words from my friend.

—*Tim Bunn PhD*
Pastor, Eagle Church of The Nazarene

Dedicated to my beautiful wife Laura, who stuck with me and encouraged me even when I was 100% wrong.

Acknowledgments

I want to express my sincere appreciation to all the people who contributed significantly to this project:

To my primary editor Angela Meuser, who provided for me the perfect balance of correction and encouragement. I look forward to our future projects.

To my friends Tim Bunn and Matt Rissell, who were the initial thorns in my side to prod me to take on this project in the first place. They both had the vision of how people were hungry for principle-based guidance.

To Randy Howard, Mark Bottles, and Les Parrott, who helped take the idea of this book and made the connections to bring it to something worth publishing.

To my wife Laura for her ongoing support and her eye for misspelled words.

To my three awesome boys Dakota, Hunter, and Logan for continuing to teach me about life and for giving me wonderful stories to share.

And finally, to all the clients and others who have allowed me into their lives and developed relationships. Their courage to share their life experiences and adversities has given others the opportunity to achieve greater potential.

Introduction

I wrapped both hands around my hot cup of coffee in an attempt to remove the winter chill as I processed what Matt said. I have known Matt for several years and we have done a fairly good job of meeting for coffee on Friday mornings when both of us happen to be in town. Our talks include many topics, ranging from marriage, parenting, spirituality, and even business decisions.

On this particular day, Matt brought up an issue that related to some potentially conflicting priorities he was facing. Matt has a strong personality and tends to appreciate directness. In fact, his natural tendency to be direct can feel somewhat like a bulldozer during a conversation. If Matt sees something that he thinks is not right, he won't hold back from boldly speaking his mind. Yet on this day, I think he was somewhat speechless when I gave him a quick and pointed answer to his perceived dilemma. He initially defended and fired a series of follow-up questions. I patiently and confidently answered Matt's objections until there was a stillness of thought in the air. After a few moments of Matt allowing the gears to crank in his mind, he sat back in his chair with a blend of defeat and enlightenment. He looked intently at me and said, "Todd, you have a gift."

It was my turn to be taken aback as I asked him what he meant. He said, "You seem to have an ability to cut directly to the key issue and give the right answer."

I responded back to him, "Matt, I don't think it's a gift, but a process." I continued, "All I do is make decisions based on principles that I already have evaluated to be true. When you were talking about your dilemma, a core issue emerged regarding aligning your priorities. Once this became evident, the solution was clear. When something is a core or foundational issue, it is more important than the specifics of your problem."

I paused briefly to allow what I said to sink in, and then continued without his response. "Once I determined what principle applied in your situation, the answer became evident without having to examine all the unique circumstances. You see, principles are consistent over time and situations; they are not contextual or swayed by unique circumstances. Every individual situation can honestly be broken down into its fundamental core issue or issues. Once you understand what principles apply, it is easy to know the right answer to the problem."

Matt sat back in his chair and after a short moment of reflection said with a great level of enthusiasm, "That's what you should write your book on—applying principles to help make decisions in life."

I gave Matt a courteous smile, thanked him for the compliment, and then our discussion drifted onto other things, and we didn't really discuss it further. Later that afternoon, however, my mind started dissecting what Matt had said. I realized people who honestly want positive change in their lives, like Matt, are literally hungry for real and meaningful answers. I believe these types of individuals do not want a bunch of rhetoric or psychobabble jargon. They are not interested in simply talking in circles around their issues—they actually want to do something to bring about real and meaningful change.

I started to think about the clients in my clinical practice and individuals I've mentored who made significant changes in their lives. The common denominator with these persons was their willingness to examine their life choices with great honesty and humility. This process of transparency was most often uncomfortable for them, but it allowed them to get to the point where they could admit how many of the things they were doing were not in line with what they wanted out of life.

People who make real changes accept that there is a right and a wrong way to think and/or do. These people either started with an existing belief, or they were willing to develop an appreciation for the need to focus on principles being a guide to their goals. This understanding allows them to become more purposeful in making right decisions.

I also thought of the significant number of people who either refused to accept principles or attempted to negotiate their way around them. These persons often justified doing what they felt like doing so they saw principle-based counsel as "narrow-minded thinking." I watched the ongoing struggle in these persons' lives. They would go month after month, year after year with no meaningful changes.

I remember listening to a man try to convince me of how going to a "swingers club" would help his relationship with his fiancé. Even though I strongly urged him to reconsider the decision because of how it would turn into a cancer in their relationship, he just continued to move forward with the plan because it was what he wanted to do. Their relationship dissolved within a few months after this "adventure." The saddest part is that I don't believe he ever connected the negative consequences of a destroyed relationship to his negative choices that violated core principles.

Many people tend to reject principles for the same reasons they reject religion. They see principles, like they see God, as nothing more than a mechanism for control. There is a strong connection between principles and God. In addition, principles are based on the fact that God has applied certain rules or laws that apply to our existence. Humans are naturally independent and rebellious to authority. If individuals choose to view principles as control, they unfortunately only hurt themselves. Principles do not need to be evaluated as control. One can choose to see principles as beneficial, somewhat like a playbook for life. If you know what works, you can intentionally perform to win.

Having spiritual beliefs does not necessarily correlate with living a successful life. One would think that persons who attended church or claimed some type of religious affiliations would be more likely to follow "Godly Principles." This can be the case, but I have counseled many Christian people who do not make decisions based on principles and then suffer the consequences of those actions. There are just as many hurting marriages and divorces with people who go to church versus those who don't.

Conversely, I have counseled many non-religious persons who do structure their lives with principles, and thus benefit from those decisions. The reason why this can happen is that principles are principles, they always work. God is no respecter of persons, which means that the same rulebook applies to everybody.

I came to the realization that Matt was right. People who are looking for real changes in their lives need the specific direction to make that happen.

This book will address principles, which I believe are based in those ultimate truths. It is difficult to talk about something being true unless we attach the concept to something that doesn't change. People change, God doesn't. Therefore, if we reason that principles or laws come from a consistent, all-powerful ruler of the universe, we can place a greater trust in those principles. They will not change based on context, motive, technology, or our emotion.

So, I started the process of writing down the things that I have been teaching my clients, individuals I've mentored, and even my own children. Very quickly I discovered that the ease I experienced in talking about these issues with people in a one-on-one setting didn't carry over to writing them down into a coherent flow of concepts. I never made the claim that I'm a natural or gifted writer, which became evident to me fairly quickly. In fact, writing is one of those things that I have always avoided and said that I wouldn't do. Thus, I began to question very early on in this process, "What did I commit myself to?" Hopefully, through the many revisions of these ideas and breaking off the rough edges with the suggestions from many people, you as the reader will feel a connection to what I am trying to teach without the sensation of being hit with a rock.

None of the principles I talk about in this book are my original ideas. These are concepts that I have learned through people much smarter than myself. I have received mentorship from personal relationships and through reading and listening to the wisdom from amazingly gifted teachers. I'm honestly not sure if there is such a thing as an original idea. An original idea is often taking the same basic concept and dressing it up in a way to get people to notice it again. This is especially true when it comes to the discussion of principles, which have been passed down from the beginning of time. I believe everything I talk about can find roots in both the old and new testaments of the Bible, but hopefully I can communicate this without sounding preachy.

I am in no way, however, attempting to offend anybody who has different beliefs than mine. The world is made up of a great diversity of spiritual belief systems. Since it is estimated that approximately 90 percent of the population believes in some manifestation of God, I hope for individuals to put the concepts that I discuss into their existing belief systems and apply it into their lives.

The way I think and present information to individuals with whom I work is through stories and analogy. I have a white board in my office and probably draw illustrations as much as I talk. I will often have clients come back and tell me that they have recreated the examples I drew out for them to several people. I encourage people to plagiarize my examples, because by them teaching these principles, it helps solidify the concepts in their own lives and it passes on truth-based concepts to others. And remember, they are not original ideas anyway. Many of the ideas I am trying to bring to words in this book are from those analogies I developed over the past few years.

Just because I am writing the book does not mean that I live a perfect life. I have successes, and I have failures. There are things I'm proud of and things I've done that I am

embarrassed to talk about. Most of the principles I address in
the following chapters are concepts that I have, at one point
or another, violated in my own life. With some of these
principles, it took me years to internalize their value and
understand how they apply to me. Much like most people, I
have gravitated towards the easy paths when navigating
through life. I too have a rebellious streak and don't want to
be "restricted" by rules. Sometimes I look over areas of my life
and wonder why I am not getting the results I want only to
discover that I am not applying the very principles that I
believe in and even teach. But know this, when I have been
successful at something, it is because I have done certain
things that brought about that success. Likewise, when I have
failed miserably, I simply wasn't doing things based in the
very principles I teach. I see myself as nothing more than a
student of what I am writing about in this book.

There are hundreds of "success" books out there, each
with their own definition of what success means. When many
people think of success, they tend to gravitate towards
material rewards, such as a high paying job or business, a
large home, the ability to travel, etc. Those things could be an
indicator of success, or they could be a façade. There are
many successful persons who have little or no material
rewards to show for it. Mother Teresa comes to mind. Success
is not defined by the attainment of anything. Simply put,
success is growth. Being a successful person is pursuing
something worthwhile in life with enough zeal that you grow
in the process.

My ultimate goal for this book is to give anybody who is
looking to grow towards his or her potential a clearly
understandable process to follow. This book is not designed
to simply motivate you to have a better life. I want this book
to be more of a study guide—something that you can pull out
for referencing a specific principle that you want to apply in
your life.

Start by reading the first section on why using principles
in our lives is important. This section lays out the foundation

for the rest of the chapters to build upon. I believe the book flows in a useful way to unlock your potential, yet the reader can flip to any single chapter and read about that principle without having to read the earlier chapters.

You were created for a purpose. You were designed with a plan that is much larger than is reflected by this moment in time. Many people are looking for the answers in their lives, which will bring about meaningful change in some area. Unfortunately, many people are not doing the right things. They might think they are on target, but find themselves circling around the same undesired results year after year. It is quite possible that these individuals are doing many things correctly, but sometimes that is simply not enough to achieve their goals. You see, people can be 90% right, yet still 100% wrong. Figuring out how to understand and correctly apply foundational principles in life makes all the difference.

Chapter 1

Finding True North
Universal Principles Can Point the Way

Policies are many, Principles are few, Policies will change, Principles never do.

— *John C. Maxwell*

Ruben and Sarah were living a life of quiet desperation. They met and married while attending college, a time for both of them that was so simple and carefree compared to the next couple decades they faced. In what seemed to be the blink of the eye, they had been married for eighteen years and their eldest of three children was already a freshman in high school.

The beginning of Ruben and Sarah's marriage was filled with huge hopes and dreams. They often stayed up till early hours of the morning talking about how they were going to conquer the world. But life happened, and their dreams were put on the back burner. When Sarah got pregnant with their first child, Ruben quit school took a job in sales "just to get them through tough times." He ended up making just enough money that he couldn't quit and go back to school to pursue his true passion of communications. He had now been with the same company for sixteen years, and his income had not kept up with the increasing cost of supporting his family.

Sarah found herself as a busy mom, and the increasing demands of her family had wiped out all of her carefree feelings. Sarah traded in her dreams of traveling the world for traveling between soccer fields on Saturday afternoons. When their youngest child started school, Sarah took a part-time job at a local clothing store to make ends meet.

Ruben and Sarah both worked hard, but it just seemed like they were not making any progress. It had been years since they felt passion for each other or for their dreams. After eighteen years of marriage, Ruben felt like he and Sarah had grown apart and simply existed in their parallel lives.

Ruben and Sarah were spending a typical Sunday afternoon working around their home when the mailman brought them a certified letter from an attorney. The letter informed Ruben that his Uncle Edward had passed away and requested Ruben to set up an appointment at Edward's home to discuss the estate.

It had been years since Ruben saw his Uncle Edward. They had pretty much lost contact after Ruben's father died a few years ago. Edward was somewhat of a reclusive man, so Ruben and his family never really had much interaction with him. Ruben's father told him that when Edward bought the home after returning from World War II, it had been a beautiful historical estate. But over the years Edward allowed the home to fall into disrepair. When driving by Uncle Edward's home a couple of years prior, Ruben had just shaken his head at how Edward had let things go.

Ruben wasn't looking forward to dealing with his Uncle Edward's estate. He imagined that since he was Edwards only living relative, he would be stuck having to go through all of Edward's junk by himself. Even though Uncle Edward's home was grand, it was so neglected that Ruben didn't believe he could even sell it.

A few days later, Ruben and Sarah pulled up to Uncle Edward's home to meet with the attorney who'd sent them the letter. The driveway was once a beautiful cobblestone

masterpiece and one could still see the pitted iron rings that
were used to tether horses a long time ago. A lack of
maintenance had allowed the weeds to come through the
cracks and conceal the beauty of the driveway. The neglected
yard surrounded them with waist deep grass and weeds. Along
the fence, one could still see straggling and overgrown rose
bushes. Ruben turned to Sarah and informed her that
Edward had once won awards for his roses. They weren't
going to win any awards the way they looked now.

As they stepped onto the front porch it sagged several
inches. Sarah clutched Ruben's arm in what he believed was
her fear that the stairs were about to give away. Ruben
stumbled when one of the weathered floorboards on the
porch caught the toe of his shoe. The screens on the windows
were dirty and falling down.

As they entered the home, the front door creaked as if
complaining about being disturbed. Sarah whispered that the
sound of the door sent chills down her spine. Walking into
the home gave Ruben the feeling of going back in time. The
furnishings appeared old and worn and a fine layer of dust
over everything dulled the colors, which had faded away over
time. Sheets covered some of the tables and chairs, which
gave Ruben the creepy feeling of walking through a haunted
house. The dirty floors groaned deeply with each of their
steps. They walked tentatively as they peered into the dark
and cluttered home. Ruben witnessed a faint shadow of a
man standing in the parlor looking at some of the books on
the shelves.

"That must be Mr. Jenkins, the attorney." Ruben
whispered to Sarah.

The man noticed Ruben and Sarah and walked across the
living room to meet them. He stretched out his hand and
gave them both a firm handshake.

"You must be Ruben and Sarah. I'm Mr. Jenkins, your
Uncle Edward's longtime attorney and friend. Sorry about
how dark it is in here, the wiring in this old house doesn't
seem to work very well. Let's go into the kitchen and talk."

As Ruben and Sarah sat down, Ruben dreaded hearing all the things he would need to attend to in order to sell Uncle Edward's estate. Ruben hoped that the sale of the home would pay off any outstanding bills because they didn't have any extra money. In fact, any amount they would have to come up with would be a burden on their family.

Mr. Jenkins started off by reminding Ruben that he was Edward's only living relative, which meant that the entire estate was his. Ruben pursed his lips and nodded his head with reluctant acknowledgement.

Mr. Jenkins went on. "You know, Ruben, although your Uncle Edward lived very meagerly, he was actually a very wealthy man."

Ruben's eyes perked up from the old papers scattered across the table.

"He was rich?" Ruben questioned with greater enthusiasm.

"Yes, quite rich." Mr. Jenkins replied. "Your uncle had been investing his money in stocks and bonds for the last sixty years. Those certificates have doubled and split many times over. I'm not exactly sure what they are all worth but it is definitely in the millions."

"Of dollars?" Sarah questioned with what seemed to be a new emotion of excitement. "Yes, millions of dollars. But like I said, I don't have all the specifics." Mr. Jenkins replied. "Your uncle was somewhat of an odd duck, and I could never get him to bring me a complete list of his investments."

Ruben questioned, "Well can't we just open up his safety deposit box and look for ourselves?"

By this time Ruben could feel Sarah's sweaty hand squeezing his. This inheritance was the answer to his prayers. He had been financially struggling for the past several years and just didn't know how they were going to make it with three kids wanting to go to college. Ruben thought that by inheriting millions of dollars, they could finally do all the things they wanted in life. Their stress would disappear, and the dreams they once embraced could finally be realized.

Mr. Jenkins responded with a sigh. "Ruben, Sarah, it's not that easy. Your uncle may have been a wealthy man who amassed a fortune, but like I said, he was also an odd duck. He didn't leave all his investments in a safety deposit box somewhere–at least not one that I know about. He entrusted me with part of his fortune but gave me specific instructions on how I should pay it out. Other pieces of his wealth are hidden from me. Your uncle knew that you were the only heirs to his estate, and he left you this map."

"He left us a map!" Sarah spoke with a challenging tone in her voice. "What are we supposed to do with a map? Look for buried treasure?"

Mr. Jenkins seemed to anticipate this reaction and remained very calm. He responded in a quiet and controlled voice, "Your uncle lived through the Great Depression, and World War II. Nothing came easy for him. He wasn't born into wealth—he created it by hard work, sacrifice, and self-discipline. He might have been a little eccentric, but he wasn't crazy. His desire was for the two of you to earn your inheritance. When I suggested that we keep his fortune in a safe place, your Uncle Edward simply said that he wasn't going to make it that easy for you."

Ruben and Sarah looked at the map and Ruben felt his heart sink in his chest. When Mr. Jenkins said that they were going to inherit millions of dollars, he thought that they would be driving that afternoon to the bank and their lives were going to change tomorrow. But when he studied the map, he realized that their appointment with the bank was going to have to wait. The map seemed to be complex and very detailed. Uncle Edward had clearly given considerable time and deep thought to his plan. Ruben allowed himself to become somewhat irritated that Uncle Edward was making them play this elaborate game for the inheritance.

Ruben thought, "Why would he do this to us? Was he simply mean or vindictive about us not coming around to see him more often?"

This map did not look like that classic image of a treasure map. It did not have landmarks with directions for a certain number of paces. It did not have a big X that marked the spot where the fortune was buried. The map had a series of instructions for Ruben and Sarah to carry out—steps that they needed to take in their lives.

The first item on the map stated: "Agree to the terms and conditions outlined by Mr. Jenkins to receive your inheritance."

Ruben and Sarah looked at each other and realized that they didn't have anything to lose. Ruben worried that Uncle Edward was, in fact, completely crazy and that there was actually no fortune at all. He realized, however, that even if that were the case, they would only lose some time and possibly be let down in their hopes and dreams. When he looked at Sarah, she nodded to him and they both signed their names on the contract with Mr. Jenkins. Mr. Jenkins nodded back and handed them a check for fifty thousand dollars.

"This is your start. Edward wanted you to know that this is real and you should be rewarded for your belief."

Ruben and Sarah sat there holding a check that was worth as much as they made in an entire year. It wasn't millions of dollars, but it still seemed like a fortune. Holding the check for fifty thousand dollars in their hands energized Ruben, and he started getting excited about uncovering and discovering the rest of their fortune.

Ruben glanced through the map and realized that the millions of dollars that awaited them were going to be found in the specific steps that Uncle Edward laid out for them. Some of the tasks required of them could be done right away, but others would take years to complete.

Mr. Jenkins shook their hands, gave them the keys to Edward's home and wished them good fortune. He said, "I'll be keeping track of your progress, and I will stay in touch." Ruben and Sarah set out on their journey to follow the instructions on their treasure map.

One of the first items on their map instructed them to go through all the boxes in the attic and donate WWII memorabilia to the local museum. When Ruben and Sarah went up into the attic, the amount of boxes and trunks that were stored there overwhelmed them. Uncle Edward, it seemed, kept everything throughout his life. They sorted through boxes for weeks. They found WWII buttons in one box and Edward's medals in another. In one of the trunks Sarah found Edward's Marine Corps uniforms. As Sarah pulled out the uniforms to hang them up, she remarked that she found something in one of the sleeves. As she dug deeper into the coat she withdrew an old and yellowed stock certificate, rolled tightly and tied with a ribbon. As she opened it up, she read aloud that the certificate was from the Ford Motor Company, and with a gasp, she said, "dated 1955." They must have stood there in the attic for thirty minutes staring at that certificate and wondering what it could possibly be worth today. Ruben realized that the only way they found the certificate was by following Uncle Edward's instructions to the letter. If they would have cut corners and only gone through the boxes looking for their prize, they would have missed it.

Other items took more time. One of the instructions was for Ruben and Sarah to clear out the front yard and bring the rose bushes back to the point of winning an award at the local fair. This item was going to take years to complete, but Ruben and Sarah discussed how they couldn't cut any corners because they might miss out on the rewards. Even though neither of them knew anything about flowers, they started to educate themselves and they went to work. After four years of effort, they finally won first place at their county fair. Within one week, they received a certified letter in the mail from Mr. Jenkins. When they opened it, the letter congratulated them for their accomplishment and had an attached check for seven hundred and fifty thousand dollars. Ruben and Sarah's hands shook. They had never held that much money before.

Ruben and Sarah spent the next twenty years completing the steps on Uncle Edward's map. They did humanitarian missions work in South America for six months, they wrote a business plan and launched a retail store, they started a local community outreach program, and they fixed up Uncle Edward's home, adding it to the town's historical registry.

Somewhere along the way, Ruben and Sarah stopped completing the items on Uncle Edward's map for the monetary rewards. They started completing the items on his map because they found value in the journey. They didn't need any more money when they were instructed to begin a foundation for a medical need they saw—they began the foundation because it was the right thing to do.

Uncle Edward might have been an odd duck, but he was a smart odd duck. His treasure map led Ruben and Sarah not only to his fortune, but also to personal and relational growth. No longer did they feel that desires of their hearts were out of reach. They were no longer living a life of quiet desperation to just "get by." From following the steps they first read on that cluttered kitchen table years ago, they learned how to be successful in all areas of their lives.

How would you respond if you were given a treasure map like Ruben and Sarah? If you knew that the treasures you have always wanted have been laid out for you, would you pursue them? Would you sign your name at the bottom of the contract and go to work, or would you sit back with doubt, fear, and skepticism?

You might be saying, "Well sure I would follow those steps if millions of dollars were waiting for me, who wouldn't? But that is a moot issue because I don't have a wealthy uncle who left me a map to his fortune."

What if you did have a map, but just didn't know it? What if the treasures that awaited you are not from someone else, but instead based on your own goals and dreams and much, much bigger than millions of dollars? And what if you will receive those treasures if you only follow the necessary steps that do, in fact exist? Would you be excited like Ruben and

Sarah? I hope that you can reach that level of excitement about your own treasures. If you can believe that those treasures exist for you, you can do what is necessary to achieve those things in your life.

You might have come to the conclusion in your life that you are not meant to be successful. This happens for so many people that you definitely won't be alone. You might be like Ruben and Sarah before they received that letter and were living a life of quiet desperation. You might feel that same lack of passion and connection with your spouse. Maybe you are struggling financially and feeling the pinch of your income not keeping up with the cost of living. Possibly you are struggling personally and do not feel good about yourself as an individual. You might have low self-esteem, depression, anxiety, high stress, or addiction problems that seem to dominate your life. You may have settled in with your life and accept a belief that the goals and dreams you once had are never going to be realized. If you believe these negative things are your destiny, I'm sorry, but I can't disagree more.

You have a potential that is beyond where you are now in your life. It might be hard to get your brain around this, but you are only operating on a fraction of your capability. If you are only currently operating at 10 percent of your potential, what dreams and goals could be realized in your future if you upped your game? Think of the limitless possibilities. What would your relationships look like? What would your finances look like? Where would your confidence be? How good would it feel to know who you are, and where you are going in life? Would you stand a little taller and smile a little brighter?

I'm not speaking hype. I'm not telling you that you can snap your fingers or wave a magic wand and bring all the desires of your heart into your life. Just like Ruben and Sarah who had to find their treasures through hard work and discipline to rules, your treasures will be found accordingly.

You have the ability to choose your future. You do not have to settle for where you are now. You have a potential that is much greater than you likely even realize. And, you have a way to take you there.

You have a map that will lead you to your potential, everybody does. This map, much like Uncle Edward's, is not as easy as using a key to unlock a safety deposit box to wealth. Your map is based on principles that have been proven to unlock everybody's potential. If a map of principles works for some, it will work for you.

The reason that principles are principles is because they are consistent. They apply regardless of the situation or the individuals who practices them. Your directions are simple, follow the principles and you will grow. As you grow, you stretch towards your potential. As you grow, the rewards of that growth will flow into you.

Principles are predictable

Principles apply to your life. It can sometimes seem like we are all alone with our particular challenges—that nobody else really shares the same struggles. I realize that you are an individual with specific circumstances and unique problems. It is normal to believe that unique people with unique problems require unique solutions. The truth is, however, that every individual is connected to the same laws that govern the physical and personal world.

Most of the time, people believe that principles exist. Once in awhile I get somebody to question, "What do you mean by 'principles' and why do you believe that they are consistent?" They point out that both people and the world we live in are constantly changing and adapting to new and different things. A logical step would be to think the principles that govern the world should also be flexible.

The world is constantly changing. People are studying and daily increasing their understanding of science, our universe, and even our personal potential. Technologies have developed in ways that just a few short years ago people commonly thought were out of our reach. Just think about how the technology of airplanes has changed over a relatively short time frame since that famous flight at Kitty Hawk in 1900. Now we have Air Force planes that fly at 80,000 feet.

Even though it seems like things are constantly changing, the laws of the universe are consistent. For example, physical laws such as gravity existed prior to Isaac Newton's experiments and theories. Even after Newton explained gravity, we didn't know how to overcome it for another two hundred years.

We, as human beings, have wanted to soar with the birds for as long as we could look up, but we couldn't just ignore gravity, become weightless, and fly like Superman. We had to understand the physical laws related to flight. Once we understood laws like Bernoulli's principle and the Coanda Effect (both laws that contribute to why an airplane wing creates lift), it was possible to build an airplane that would overcome the law of gravity. These physical laws have also been around since the beginning of time. It just took us up to the last century to understand and apply them.

Our personal lives are connected to our business lives. We cannot separate them because it is more convenient.

Much like how physical laws have been present for all time, so have laws that apply to humans and human interactions. When we speak about laws that apply to humans, we often use the term "principle." Just because we use the word "principle" doesn't mean that it is less consistent or powerful than a law. Principles are not theory. Principles have been consistently shown throughout history to always hold constant.

There is a natural human tendency to accept physical laws, but resist principles. People tend to believe they are smart enough to make their own decisions on what is right. Even the most intelligent and logical humans use emotions to guide their philosophies of life. People reason that they can do what they feel is right to get the results they want. This attitude often pays off in the short term, which gives people the impression that their reasoning is right. But a violation of a principle always eventually catches up and no longer works.

For example, a husband might think that he will feel strong if he is controlling and demanding towards his wife. This might work for a while as his wife gives in to his dominating behavior. But nobody likes to be dominated, and his wife eventually loses respect for this man and distances herself from him. As his wife pulls back and their relationship falls apart, this man no longer feels strong and in control of his life. Thus, his short-term emotional-based strategy did not lead to his long-term goal.

People also like to apply situational ethics as a way to justify our desires without consequences. This simply doesn't work. We can't have ethics in only one area of life. We either approach life with ethics or we don't. Our personal lives are connected to our business lives. We cannot separate them because it is more convenient.

If you have children, I am fairly positive that you expect them to act on principles. Imagine if you had a son who tried to convince you that his drug use was not a problem because all the kids are doing it, and he felt like it was in his control. The reasons he used are situational and emotional. Regardless of his reasons, I believe you would still see his behavior as problematic. This is because you probably have a principle-based belief that drugs are bad.

It is much easier for us to see how principles apply towards other people. But remember, what applies to one person applies to all persons.

You might wonder where all these physical and personal principles come from. Just look at the consistency, complexity, and the way all these laws work together. They are clearly not random occurrences. For principles to work the way they do, they had to be designed with some type of plan in mind, much like how an architect lays out the designs for a building.

I believe that many people have a conceptualization of God as some type of puppet master, sitting up in Heaven making minute decisions about every facet of our lives. I'm not trying to speak for God, but it just seems like such a level of involvement is unnecessary when so much of the universe can be run off of established laws. For example, the law of gravity: God doesn't have to decide if a person who trips is going to fall to the ground or float, that law is already predetermined. The laws of gravity and inertia and centrifugal motion (and probably some other ones) keep our earth spinning and traveling on a trajectory around the Sun. God doesn't have to keep things moving, he has a series of laws that simply take care of it.

Think of if it with the analogy of a computer programmer who writes code. Would she write a new piece of code every time she wanted something to happen, then erase it only to write it again? Or, would she write a code to produce a specific result each time something happened? The logical thing to do is to write one code that would handle an event every time it occurred. So, every time you push the big button in the bottom middle of the keyboard, the cursor moves one space. Once that piece of code is in place, the corresponding results will always be reliable. We come to rely on this predictability to function in life.

So doesn't it make sense that there are also created codes or laws that govern all things in this universe? I see principles as a system of codes, by which to live and function in our lives. God is not looking to punish and torment you through a system of rules and controls. He simply crafted the laws that bring about your own consequences for the decisions you make. These laws restrict you, but they also allow you to play the game of life—and to win. Such laws are what make up the individual steps on your treasure map to success. Just like Uncle Edward created steps on the treasure map for Ruben and Sarah to help them find their treasures, principles exist for you to find your treasures.

Do you believe that you have a potential that is greater than what you are realizing right now in your life? Do you think it is possible that you are only operating on a fraction of your capabilities? If you knew that you could increase your efficiency in life and that would lead you to the treasures of your heart, wouldn't your thoughts begin to race? All of a sudden, those former dreams and goals that you believed were out of reach could come back into focus. You wouldn't have to settle for the life you have right now. The stress you feel does not have to be there forever. Think about the possibilities of what you could accomplish in the many areas of your life.

Why don't you learn how to make a life for yourself instead of just making a living or getting by with the life you have? Don't live a settle-for life. If you choose to accept mediocrity, you will never do what it takes to hold out for greatness.

These laws restrict you, but they also allow you to play the game of life— and to win.

Do not fall into the trap of thinking that being successful is not your destiny. Success is not something that is decided for you. Achieving success is not based on an unknown formula of luck, talent, or fate. The fact of the matter is that achieving success in anything is based on doing the right things. The good thing about following principles in your life is that the principles of being successful do not change. Principles are like the North Pole, it's always in the same place on the planet. If you use a compass to navigate through life, the needle will always point in the same direction.

Believing in ultimate truth is not always the most popular idea because it seems limiting and even judgmental. When we define what is correct; we automatically define what is wrong. Most people don't like these kinds of limitations placed on their lives. The truth is, however, that principles are only judgmental if you use them to judge others. If someone refuses to follow a compass when they are lost in the woods;

that is their choice. You do not need to feel the responsibility to correct their thinking. The way you apply principles in your own life is simply to evaluate your own progress and understand that if you discipline yourself to use principles you won't get as lost as often.

You have everything you need to be successful in any area of your life because you can follow a map. Your success is not based on anything that is outside of your control. Your success is based on your willingness to discipline yourself to do the right things in life. If you have succeeded in anything, it is simply because you did the things that led to that result. If you are failing in life, it is simply because you are doing the wrong things. As harsh as this statement sounds, this could be a freedom experience for you because it drops the limitations off of your life. Just because you have failed at something in the past doesn't mean that you cannot turn that around. Whatever you want to improve in, be it your finances, your marriage, your mood, or your physical fitness, you can set your sights on your goals and begin to follow the proven path towards success in those areas. Success is only one decision away for you. Decide well.

Take Away Discussion Questions

1. In what ways can you identify with Ruben and Sarah's life of quiet desperation?

2. What goals and dreams did you have in the past that you haven't thought of in awhile?

3. Are there areas in your life where you think you have settled for mediocrity?

4. How has the stress of your challenges negatively impacted your life?

5. If a treasure map were presented to you, would you respond with excitement or doubt?

6. God created laws that govern the universe as well as human interaction. What are your thoughts about why God created these laws?

7. It takes a leap of faith to follow principles when our emotions often direct us the other way. Is your tendency to approach principles with faith or fear?

8. I defined success as growth. How do you define success and why?

9. What areas in your life do you believe you could achieve a greater potential?

10. You are only operating on a fraction of your potential. What do you think would change in your life if you increased your belief and effort?

11. The idea of dreaming again can be an exciting process. What feelings come up for you when you allow yourself to think about those dreams again?

12. What is the one thing you are going to take away from this chapter and put into practice in your life, starting now?

Chapter 2

Packing Your Bags
The Application of Principles in Your Life

> *Man's greatness consists in his ability to do and the proper application of his powers to things needed to be done.*
>
> — *Frederick Douglass*

Harland David Sanders dropped out of school in the seventh grade and ran away from home and an abusive stepfather. He enlisted in the Army and attempted a wide variety of careers throughout his lifetime. At the age of forty Sanders started cooking chicken and serving customers in a living quarters area of his gas station business. When he ran out of room in his home, Sanders set up a small restaurant in a roadside motel. He probably would have stayed in that location for the rest of his life, but in 1956 a new highway bypassed his restaurant and customer base dropped. Saunders auctioned off his property for seventy-five thousand dollars to cover his debts. At the age sixty-six, and for the most part broke, Sanders found himself at a loss of direction for what was next.

Having a monthly social security income of one hundred five dollars, Harland "Colonel" Sanders started traveling the United States with his pressure cooker and secret recipe. Most of the quality restaurants he called upon, threw him out in the street. They told him, "We already know how to cook chicken." But Colonel Sanders didn't quit. Even when all the evidence showed that he was failing, he kept going to new restaurants in different towns. The small, mom and pop type establishments were where he started getting some success. Colonel Sanders made a deal with these restaurants to give them his secret recipe, and in return they paid him back one nickel per person.

Colonel Sander's perseverance paid off. By 1960 he had four hundred franchisees and the image of his face to sell chicken had gained national exposure. Three years later he made three hundred thousand dollars in a single year. In 1964, he sold the company for two million dollars plus a lifetime annual salary of forty thousand dollars to be the company spokesperson. So, a man whom most considered to be at the age of retirement, went from broke and dependent on government support to be a multimillionaire in less than ten years. And, furthermore, he did it by taking what he knew worked in his hometown and using it to expand his vision across the country.

Many people who have achieved great things in life appear to have overnight success. This is because we don't tend to look at the underlying process and struggle that they went through for years. Most successful people will honestly inform you that they have missed more goals than they have hit. This means that they have failed more times than they have succeeded. The fact they are still standing at the end of the match is simply because they refused to stay down each time they were knocked to the mat.

When we look at the successes of others, we don't see the times where the person was putting forth positive energy, but not getting a return. Because most people don't see the full journey of others, they don't have a realistic expectation for their own successes. Since they don't understand these principles of growth, they quit before their dreams and desires can be realized.

The more you believe in yourself and the fact that God wants you to grow to your potential, the greater your results will be. Your willingness to follow established laws will take you further than any amount of talent or skill ever will. You have what it takes to be successful because you can learn about principles and how to apply them to your journey. In fact, I know you have already proved this to be true at some point in your life. All you need to do is pack your bags for the right trip.

Strength comes from conviction

Principles give us strength because they allow us to believe in something that is greater than ourselves. If we allow the rules that we live our lives by to be variable, this promotes skepticism and doubt in everything. This is not good for us. We need to move away from self-definition of what is right and wrong.

Have you ever seen small children playing a game in which they evolve the rules during the game? They can get pretty creative. In the heat of being pursued, a child might say, "You can't tag me because I am touching this chair; this chair is base!" Then the next child claims that he was tagged when he had already given the "time out" sign. The rules tend to escalate in their complexity to the point of the game doesn't make sense anymore. Ultimately, the children fight more than they enjoy the activity.

My second son, Hunter, does this quite well. He has a very quick and creative mind and leads both his brothers in mind-twisting illogical arguments. For example, Hunter posed the question to his younger brother, Logan, "What is the fastest animal?" When Logan says "A cheetah," Hunter responds with "Wrong. It's a dog riding in a car on the freeway?" This type of question-answer forum can go on for hours and last much longer than Laura and my tolerance levels. It is frustrating because there are no rules that govern Hunter's process, so nobody can ever get the right answers to his questions. No matter what is said, the rules of the game change so Hunter can be right.

If we attempt to define the principles of how we live our lives by making them up as we go, we will get in trouble. Determining what is right and

It is impossible to stand for everything without ending up standing for nothing.

wrong based on our own logic or what happens to feel good in the moment is risky business. When we allow ourselves to move away from established principles we run the risk of gravitating towards a society where anybody could potentially justify anything. This takes us towards an acceptance of victimization and external blame for our problems.

Could you imagine following a map that constantly changed? Each time you came to a checkpoint, the path switched directions. You would probably throw it out the window because it is important for you to experience progress towards your goals. A map that is always different at each turn will keep the reader lost.

Some people argue that principles are limiting to human creativity and used by individuals or groups as a mechanism for control. I will be the first to admit that human beings have used principles, such as biblical statements, to promote their own self-interest and control others. But before you throw the baby out with the bathwater, let's try and separate out the intention of principles from the misuse of them.

When we stand for something that is based in truth, we are claiming that there is a right and wrong. This is not popular. If we stand on a principle that something is right, it means the opposite of that principle is wrong. People do not want to evaluate what they think or do as wrong. So, they resist accepting those labels because they don't want to feel bad.

"But if I take a stand for things I believe in, I might offend somebody and they wouldn't like me. I don't want to be mean or critical. There is already too much hate in the world."

This is absolutely true. It is much easier to go through life embracing everything that comes along. After all, we don't want to be seen as judgmental or superior. But the truth is, it is impossible to stand for everything without ending up standing for nothing. If a person doesn't stand for something, people may like him, but they won't tend to respect him. I tell my boys all the time "If you have to choose between being liked and being respected, do the things that will produce respect from the people you respect." Respect is a much more long-range accomplishment. It will bring much more success into one's life that being liked ever will.

Besides, following principles is not about judgment—it is about effectiveness. You and I don't need to judge anybody as being bad or good. I think we can get in trouble when we start believing that we are better than others because of what we believe. We can say that somebody is honest or dishonest, but it is important to not extend that concept to an evaluation of that person being either good or bad. I remember a story of Jesus coming upon a mob, who were about to stone a prostitute to death. Jesus simply told them that the person with no sin in their own lives should be the one to cast the first stone. This bit of truth had the effect of disbanding the mob. They dropped their rocks on the ground and walked away.

Likewise, there are people who focus heavily on the fact that they are good or right in their choices, yet have very little results to show for it. Dave is a Christian man who constantly verbally berated his wife because she was not following what the Bible told her to do. Dave saw himself as good because he was referencing Biblical scriptures. He might have been right in his evaluation of the content, but his approach with his wife did not produce any positive results.

We can get away from judgmental thinking when we get away from righteous attitudes. Instead of thinking what is "right," we need to evaluate something we do as either "effective" or "ineffective" as taking us closer to our goals. Focus on being effectiveness over being righteous.

Principles will work if you work those principles. But the key is in the application. To understand the application of principles, all principles need to be placed on a continuum of two opposite extremes. On one end is rigidity and legalism. People who camp out in this extreme often stand for the right things, but lose their effectiveness in their application. If someone takes a good principle, but then judges others who think or believe differently, the underlying principle is often lost.

Focus on being effective over being righteous.

A friend of mine, who is a retired pastor, was reading a book on Buddhist philosophy one morning when I stopped into Starbucks. We started talking about how much he was enjoying the book and how Buddhist teachings on humanity are very good in principle. I not only agreed with him, I suggested that if more Christian people lived their lives with the simplicity of love and harmony, like the Buddhists' believe, they would be closer to what Jesus actually taught. But unfortunately, many westernized religious people get so caught up in the doctrine of what they believe to be true that they lose the underlying principle of that value.

Jesus taught this in the parable of the good Samarian. A man walking down a road and minding his own business was attacked by thieves and left for dead. Several men passed by, but did not help the man. One of these men was a Rabbi, who passed the man because his "law" told him that touching a dead man will separate him from God. Then came along a man from Samaria, who although thought to be an enemy by culture, picked up the man, took him to an inn, and paid for his stay. Jesus simply asked, "Which one of these men showed love towards his fellow man?" It clearly wasn't the one who became so rigid with his "law" that he lost sight of the greater principle of love.

On the other end of this continuum is what I term "tolerationism", or an acceptance of anything and everything as okay. We can attempt to convince ourselves that that there is no right or wrong, but the challenge is we might engage in thinking or acting that simply won't produce results. I have found that the truth of most things have been found to be somewhere in the balance of most continuums. Both extremes tend to lose the core value of the principle.

The principles are right, yet people don't always apply them correctly. For example, if a medical student learns anatomy and techniques of surgery, she can take that knowledge and apply it to help many people. That is a good application of knowledge. Another student in her class, however, could take the same knowledge and use it to kill people with greater efficiency. So if we discover that a serial killer went to the best medical school in the nation, do we claim that the knowledge that was provided to him was bad? Of course not. We understand that the principle knowledge was good and designed to heal, the application of that knowledge used to hurt was bad.

I look at principles in the same light. Principles are in place in this universe for your benefit. Everything that we deal with in this world has some form or function and is in place for some purpose. I don't totally understand why Noah didn't swat those two mosquitoes, but I remind myself that I don't know everything. Unfortunately, people have a tendency to abuse things that are intended for good. I don't believe we will ever remove that from society. The underlying principle, however, is still good regardless if people screw it up or not.

The principles I am sharing throughout this book are for you personally, not a tool to change others. You will have to evaluate the principles that resonate with your life and choose to either apply them or not apply them for yourself. This book is not about learning things so you can go around telling people how to think or what to do.

The way I look at the treasure map of principles is that it is better to be informed than it is to be ignorant. At least if you know what the right answers are, you can approach life with more purpose and direction. If you are unaware of a principle, you will tend to stumble through life. You might do the right things, but there is just as much of a chance that you would do the wrong things. Ignorance of a law will not insulate anybody from the effects of that law. A person doesn't have to believe in gravity to fall from a tree.

Principles are greater than talent

"But Todd, not everybody can be successful. Some people just have talent and some don't."

It is absolutely the case that certain things can come easier to some individuals. I remember when I was in high school and how grades never came easy for me. I didn't realize it at the time, but a touch of dyslexia made reading and processing information difficult. I had a high school friend named Doug who never seemed to take school seriously, yet he got straight A's. Doug was a very smart guy. If an accident hadn't taken his life in his early twenties, I believe he would have fulfilled his dreams of running for the Presidency. In high school Doug impressed me with his ability to simply listen to the teachers, glance through a book, and never studying to ace the tests. This was never the case for me.

I married a woman with very similar giftedness. Laura is a voracious reader and has a talent for language. She is constantly reading books or articles and complaining that editors aren't doing their jobs effectively due to the frequent spelling errors she finds. I am still not a fast reader. It takes my brain about three times longer than hers to process information. If we ever read together, it can be a frustrating experience when I hear her turning to the next page when I am only through one paragraph. She is gifted with words and I am the one writing the book, sometimes life just doesn't make sense.

Based on how poorly I did in high school, it would have been a fair prediction that I wouldn't have done well in college. But in college, I had something I didn't have in high school—a specific goal to accomplish. I knew that other students were intellectually and academically more gifted than me, but I believed I could outwork them. By the time I started college, I had a clearly mapped out a plan to get my PhD in psychology. Good thing I was fairly naïve, because I never considered that I wasn't capable of achieving it. I actually recall thinking, "Psychologists just listen to people all day long, how hard could that be?"

When I set out on that journey, I learned that to get into a PhD program I would have to have close to a 4.0 grade point average in college. That became my focused goal. I just started taking the necessary classes and doing whatever was needed to get an "A." College was not a social experience for me. If I had been single and living in a fraternity during college, I probably wouldn't have had the focus to get the performance I needed.

Success is not a specific destination— success is growth.

So the things needed to perform in school were not talents for me, yet I was able to achieve some degree of success in school. This is not because I'm somehow special or uniquely chosen for success. I was able to achieve in school simply because I applied principles consistent with success in that area. Now, I didn't understand that this was what I was doing at the time. Nobody was counseling me to discipline myself and get single-minded on my goal. My focus was simply based on what I believed I needed to do. Fortunately, I did the right things.

"I'm not sure I believe that concept. What about somebody who has a goal of being a professional basketball player, but they don't have an ounce of talent? They can't possibly follow principles of success to lead them to their dreams."

This is absolutely true. It's a good thing that I never had a dream to be a professional basketball player. The NBA doesn't often recruit 5' 10" players who can't move the ball, can't shoot, and can't jump. If being a basketball player were my only version of success I would be disappointed and quite possibly see myself as a failure in life.

What this question really addresses is how we define success for ourselves. We have to be careful that we don't lock our sights so tightly onto one thing that all we can see is failure if we miss it. Remember, success is not a specific destination—success is growth.

The self-disciplined will succeed greater than the talented when the talented won't discipline themselves.

If a person had the dream of playing basketball, but didn't have the necessary talent, they might not ever be an NBA player. However, for someone who loves basketball, there are many other great goals to pursue within that passion. A person could become a referee, a coach, or even a sports news reporter. The bottom line— talents can separate people out when it comes to specific results, but they are not necessary for growth.

Kathy is a woman in her forties who has a lifetime struggle with self-esteem, mostly based on a problem with fairly significant dyslexia. Kathy struggled throughout her entire life with reading and writing, and she was constantly embarrassed that someone would notice this problem. Kathy had only brothers, who all seemed to excel academically. She constantly compared how successful they were and how her life was miserable. Kathy always connected her inability to read with perceived low intelligence. Even more unfortunate was that Kathy's overall view of her chances to be successful in anything were based in her reading and writing ability. Therefore, according to her, she could never be successful.

Through many discussions with Kathy it became quite apparent that she was a naturally gifted leader. She saw herself, however, as "just an employee at a cafeteria," but Kathy was actually leading the entire crew. All the other employees came to Kathy—even her supervisor sought her out for advice on management decisions. When it was pointed out that she really had a talent for leadership, Kathy denied this conclusion with the reasoning that she was not smart.

"How could a person lead when they can't even read?" she would ask. Kathy seemed to get frustrated that I was not validating her sense of lifelong failure based on her dyslexia. When I encouraged her to not allow her dyslexia to limit her, she acted like I just didn't get it.

Kathy had focused all her energy on one version of success. She wouldn't allow herself to see beyond the one thing that was, in fact, a weakness in her life. This narrow view of her abilities caused her to miss the big picture of what her potential truly was. It was as if Kathy was on her journey down the path of life, and she saw a gold coin up in a tree that was out of her reach. But Kathy stayed there, focusing on that one coin instead of understanding that there many coins down the path ahead of her. All she needed to do was focus on growth instead of a particular result.

Success in some areas will always come easier for some people. Talent does play a part in how easy something might be for a person. You have talents that make certain things you do easier for you. The thing with talents, however, is that we tend to take them for granted. You honestly probably minimize the things that come natural to you, while you hold in high esteem things that other people do well.

Many talented people simply do not work hard enough to pursue their dreams and goals in life. Their talent allows them to "cruise" through life with some degree of success, without ever having to make the hard and self-disciplining types of decisions that will ultimately lead toward their potential. Therefore, the self-disciplined will succeed greater than the talented when the talented won't discipline themselves.

Because of individual strengths and weaknesses, it might take you longer to get the results you want, but you can still get there. Ruben and Sarah weren't talented at growing roses. It took them four years to learn what they needed to accomplish that goal. It all comes down to a basic truth, if you follow the correct directions on the map, you will also have your individual treasures.

Talent could possibly make that journey easier, but that talent can also get in the way. Never tell yourself that you cannot achieve something in your life because you don't have the natural talent or giftedness. These qualities are not a requirement for your success. The only talent that you need to develop is how to follow directions.

You have what it takes to be successful

Tim sat across from me with a huge smile on his face. He looked like he had just found the pot of gold at the end of the rainbow. Tim is a close friend and pastor of a large and growing church. He is one of those guys who is loved by everybody who meets him, which is one of the reasons why he is so successful as a senior pastor.

On this day, Tim informed me that he applied something we talked about a few weeks earlier and reported feeling successful in two areas of his life. He had a confident and pleased look on his face and he appeared eager to share his insight and results. Tim stated that he had lost about 20 pounds, which he had wanted to do for several years. Tim also said that he started approaching his staff in a way that produced better results. I asked Tim what it was that he did differently?

He said, "Todd, you told me that all success is based on following established principles. You said that most people are successful in at least one area in their lives, but this does not mean that they are successful in all areas of their lives." He continued, "This was huge for me because I realized that if I struggled in some areas in my life, I didn't have to live that way. If I was successful in an area of my life, it was because I was doing the right things there. If I was not successful in something, it was because I wasn't doing the right things. So, to be successful, I simply had to apply the right principles."

Tim went on to describe how he was able to identify a couple areas in his life where he believed he was successful. The church where he was the pastor had grown significantly with his leadership. Tim also looked to his marriage and family and could see that he had done many right things there, as well.

Tim understood that his successes in his life were not based on luck, chance, or fate, but were based on choices and behaviors that were within his control.

Tim got it. The look that I saw in his eyes was hope. Hope that he could change something in his life that had previously seemed overwhelming and hopeless. Hope that he had everything he needed to make his life better. He had already proved to himself that he could be successful in one place. That gave him confidence that he could be successful in any area of his life. He only had to transfer the principles.

Think about how this applies in your own life. If you knew that anything you hoped for was within your grasp, how would you feel? Encouraged? Excited? Energized? I hope that you can have those feelings. You probably had that excitement in your youth before you became discouraged through your failures. Don't you want to feel that hope and excitement again?

It can sometimes seem that success is an exclusive club, to which we are not invited. The truth is, you have within you everything you need to be successful. I am confident you have already applied those principles in your life somewhere and got the corresponding results. Maybe you did well in school, or in sports. Maybe you are the life of the party and you naturally connect with others. Maybe you give your best when you bake a cake. Or you could be the person who has the "Midas Touch" when it comes to money or business. Most individuals take whatever they are good at for granted and think that it doesn't count because it is easy. The ease of your results doesn't matter. It still counts because you did the right things. You have the results, because whether you recognize it or not, you followed principles.

"But I know for a fact that being successful just comes easier for some people. I have tried to read books on being successful before. It just doesn't seem to work for me."

Many people get to feeling down because they are not where they want to be in life. They might be controlled by food, alcohol, or other addictions. They might not have the relationships they desire in their hearts. Or they might not have the success in business or finances that they seek. They get down because they know they are not where they want to be, but the idea of change is often overwhelming.

It's been said that the greatest fear of man is the fear of change. People resist change for a variety of reasons. First, people like the feeling of familiar. The idea of change is a threat to feelings in our lives that we don't want to lose. Second, people think that change must be drastic to bring about different results. This follows the old "how do you eat an elephant" question. If we see something too big or ominous, it can feel overwhelming to even know where to start. And finally, some people believe that change is not possible for them. These persons mistakenly believe that even if they did change it wouldn't make any difference. In short order, they shoot themselves in the foot before they even have a chance to run the race of life.

Change equals different and different equates to feeling uncomfortable. Individuals become quite comfortable with how they approach life, even if it doesn't work. What complicates this further is how a particular strategy can seem to work in some areas, but clearly doesn't work elsewhere. A man, for example, can be very controlling in running his business, which might work for him, but that same strategy in running his home will backfire.

I recently used an analogy with a man who was fearful of losing his sense of power, control, and security if he changed. Imagine you are a piece of iron in the shape of a sword. Change doesn't mean that you will morph into something like wood or straw, becoming soft or ineffective. Change is the process of taking the material that you already are and removing the impurities, shaping you to become sturdier, and sharpening you to become more effective. But imagine if the piece of iron could talk: "You mean that I'm going to get pounded and some of my metal will be removed; that sounds like I will be weaker." People think about changing themselves in the same way. "If I change to what my wife needs from me, I will be a weak and ineffective pushover." The reality is the shaping and sharpening process of change makes one stronger and more effective at getting the things we ultimately want out of life.

You will not lose the basis of your metal. You will not become something or someone you don't respect if you change. You do not have to become somebody or something that is not real. You are only going to remove the parts of you that don't work or drag you down.

People sometimes feel overwhelmed because they believe that they will have to change so significantly to reach their goals that it almost seems impossible. The truth is, you don't have to change everything or change radically. Bringing about real and lasting change in one's life is closer than most people think. You will not have to change 90 percent of what you do in life to achieve your treasures.

Bringing about real and lasting change in one's life is closer than most people think.

In Pastor Tim's case, he didn't have to turn his life upside down to achieve his goals. He didn't have to exercise all the time. He simply disciplined himself for three hours of exercise per week. Three hours out of the 168 hours in a week is only 1.8 percent of the week. Tim didn't have to stop eating or eat only cardboard food bars. He had to eliminate the extra eating and not give in to the temptation for eating for the wrong reasons. Tim openly admitted that the difference between the amount of food that he was eating before and after his decision to lose weight wasn't that much. Tim ate a half of portion instead of filling his plate—the same size of meal as his wife. Tim admitted that he didn't feel like he had to give up that much to achieve the results he was seeking, he just needed to discipline himself in the emotional decision related to food.

Who you are is not that far off from whom you can become through good and consistent decisions. In fact, it is very likely that you only need to change the 10 percent of things that are holding you back. It is the small things that you can change consistently in your life that will make all the differences.

Some people believe that changing themselves is either impossible, or even if they did somehow manage to change, it wouldn't affect the poor results they get out of life. This type of people has a fatalistic view of themselves and of life. These persons are like the woman, Kathy, who saw her dyslexia as impossible to change and the factor that would always keep her from achieving any worthwhile goals in life.

Persons who don't see the power to change their own lives often look to external factors for change. They wait for others to change or make things better for them, or they wait for luck to change in their lives.

I was speaking with a woman once who said, "I really need to change my life, maybe I should start playing the lottery." A lottery ticket is an attempt to change one's life, simply by luck—a very long shot at luck. But, the more I tried to get her to understand that she could be successful by following principles in her life, she kept going back to results being associated with luck. What she didn't seem to understand was that focusing on buying a lottery ticket and getting more money with luck was actually giving up on herself and her ability to make her life successful.

One might say, "Well Todd, somebody has to win, it may as well be me. I feel lucky."

A person doesn't win a lottery game because she is lucky, she wins because she had a 1:1,357,974 chance of winning. Likewise, random bad things don't happen to a person because of bad luck, they happen because a certain percentage of bad things happen in life.

Living by the belief of luck is a losing proposition. Every lottery winner ends up losing because they didn't have to develop the principles in their lives to be able to manage wealth. Even though they become rich financially, they continue to live poorly. Many who get wealth easily, lose it as fast as they get it.

Discomfort is confirmation that things are changing in your life.

But more importantly, even when people win their "treasures," they don't win in life because they didn't create their own success. Would you want your child to get an "A" in school because good grades were randomly given out, or would you want him or her to earn it? Doesn't the same principle apply in your own life? If you somehow get the rewards of success without the necessary work, you will miss out on the greatest rewards in life, the satisfaction that you made it happen.

Watch your excuses for not changing. You have what it takes to be successful in any area because somewhere in your life you have followed principles that led to your existing successes. If you don't change to follow principles in areas where you are not successful, nothing will change. Changing the things in your life that are holding you back is within your grasp. You will only become stronger and more effective if you remove the pieces of you that simply don't work. This is always uncomfortable, but discomfort is confirmation that things are changing in your life.

Take Away Discussion Questions

1. Having conviction about principles will make you feel stronger. Why do you this would be the case?

2. Many people reject principles and engage in the same non-productive patterns in life. What are some of the perceived challenges that keep people from accepting principles?

3. Conviction of principles can be misused. Are there examples in your life where principles were used to justify criticism or control?

4. How does one follow principles, yet find balance between legalism and tolerationism?

5. What is the value of choosing effectiveness over righteousness?

6. What areas in your life do you believe you haven't had the talent to succeed?

7. Principles are greater than talent. Where has this concept proved to be true in your experience?

8. You have what it takes to succeed. You have proven this somewhere. What are some areas in your life where you have demonstrated successful results?

9. Where are you going to apply your successful principles next?

10. What is the one thing you are going to take away from this chapter and put into practice in your life, starting now?

Chapter 3

You Have to Dig Deep to Build Big
The Principle of Character

*If once you forfeit the confidence of your fellow
citizens, you can never regain their respect and esteem.*

— *Abraham Lincoln*

A Chinese emperor was growing old and knew that it was
time to choose his successor. Instead of following tradition,
he called all the young men in the kingdom together. He
said, "It has come time for me to step down and to choose the
next Emperor. I have decided to choose one of you to
succeed me. I am going to give each of you a single seed. I
want you to go home, plant the seed, water it and come back
here twelve months from today with what you have grown
from this seed. I will then judge the plants that you bring to
me, and the boy I choose will be the next Emperor."

A twelve year-old boy by the name of Ling attended that
day and he, like the others, received a seed. He ran home and
with great excitement told his mother the whole story. That
same day Ling planted his precious seed in one of his
mother's most beautiful pots. He took good care of what had
been entrusted to him.

After a few weeks some of the other boys began to talk about their plants beginning to grow. Ling kept checking his pot every day, but never saw any growth. He felt like a failure and believed that he had done something to kill his seed. Ling grew with embarrassment regarding his pot and didn't talk with the other boys as they bragged on their plants.

Finally, the twelve months had passed and all the boys of the kingdom brought their plants to the Emperor for inspection. Ling told his mother that he didn't want to go to the ceremony because he had failed, but she encouraged him to go, and to take his pot. Ling felt sick to his stomach, but he knew he had to be honest about what happened. So, Ling picked up his pot filled with lifeless dirt and took it to the palace.

When Ling arrived, he witnessed the very beautiful and large plants the other boys grew. Ling put his pot on the floor. Many of the other kids laughed at him. His shame about his failure caused him to slip to the back of the crowd.

When the Emperor arrived, he walked through the grand room and greeted the young men. Ling tried to hide in the back and out of sight

"My, what great plants you have grown," said the emperor." The Emperor kept walking past all the wonderful flowers and bushes. Ling looked up from barren dirt and made eye contact with the emperor. The emperor ordered his guards to bring Ling and his pot to the front. Ling thought he was about to be ridiculed in front of his friends. When Ling got to the front, the Emperor looked down at him and asked his name.

"My name is Ling," he replied.

The Emperor looked at Ling, and shocked the crowd by saying, "Behold your new Emperor. His name is Ling!"

Through Ling's fear of his own failure he didn't even process what the emperor had said. It took Ling several moments and hearing the cheers from his friends to comprehend what just happened. He thought, "I couldn't even grow my seed. How could I be the new Emperor?"

Then the Emperor spoke, "One year ago today, I gave everyone here a seed. I told you to take the seed, plant it, water it, and bring it back to me today. But I gave you all boiled seeds, which would not grow. All of you, except Ling, have brought me trees and plants and flowers. When you found that the seed would not grow, you substituted another seed for the one I gave you. Ling was the only young man with the courage and honesty to bring me a pot with my seed in it. Therefore, it is he who will be the new Emperor."

Don't you just love stories like this? We love the idea of people doing the honorable things in life and be recognized and praised for their character.

Character is found in our core

Transparency and character go hand in hand. When something is transparent, you can see right through it, nothing is hidden. If you have a clear glass filled with water, you can easily see if your drink is dirty. In my home we call this process "checking for floaties" and usually it follows drinking after a child.

We also need to strive for that same transparency to show our personal quality. When people see your outside, they also need to see all the way down to your core. Transparency will free you from the bondage of your weaknesses, and it will allow others to trust and believe in you.

Being transparent is not an easy process. If we allow ourselves to be transparent, that means we will end up showing areas of ourselves that we don't want to face and don't want others to see. Most people spend the majority of their lives trying to cover up things in their life that they feel are negative or embarrassing.

One of things that I was embarrassed about for many years was my reading and spelling ability. I can remember when I was in junior high school and saying silent prayers that the teacher wouldn't call on me to read aloud to the class. When I realized that I struggled with reading and writing, I concluded that I was not as smart as other students. I didn't want to feel inferior, so whatever I did, I couldn't let other people see that I wasn't smart. As a strategy to feel better about myself, I avoided situations where I would be "found out" and potentially be made fun of.

When you feel like you have to cover up something in your life, that secret will control you.

Believe it or not, I carried the insecurity of my intelligence up until a few short years ago. I continue to misspell common words, like "spouse," even though I have written that particular word literally thousands of times. I sometimes start to write "S-p-o-u" and then for the life of me, I can't see in my mind's eye if the next letter is an "s" or a "c." Spell-check in word processors is one of the greatest advancements of our modern culture. Because of my poor spelling and legibility, I avoided writing in front of others. I feared that I would lose credibility with people if they saw me misspell familiar words. But that lack of transparency in my life was bad for me. When you feel like you have to cover up something in your life, that secret will control you.

I eventually came to the realization that I didn't feel good about myself when I tried to hide my weaknesses. So, I started being open about my struggle. I started joking with people when I was standing up at my white board and was at a loss when spelling a word. It took me a long time, but once I refused to hide my spelling challenges, I became less embarrassed, and it no longer held the same power over me. When I became transparent with that perceived weakness, it freed me. I came to the realization that people can be smart in different ways—that my dyslexia did not define my intelligence or ability.

When we become transparent based on quality principles in our lives, we start building character. We measure character in others by the consistency in which a person demonstrates those principle values in his or her life.

Character is found in our core because the core is more accurate than what is on the surface. We can craft our outward presentation, but whatever is in our core will eventually come bubbling to the surface. If we don't have a principle in our core, there is no way we can ever be consistent as we navigate through life.

Imagine we are talking about the dirt we have in our back yard. If we buried a bunch of toxic waste in 50-gallon drums in our back yard, we could cover it up with good soil and even plant grass seed. After a season, we could fertilize, water, and manicure that back lawn so that it was the prize yard in the entire city. But what happens with that toxic waste? Well, it has a way of seeping up through the ground and the lawn starts to die. As the lawn dies, the easiest thing to do is bringing in fresh topsoil and reseeding the lawn. The lawn would look good for another season or two before the toxic core began to seep through and destroy once again. We could literally continue to go through that same process every couple of years for the rest of our lives, yet never fix the problem. The only way to keep fertile ground in the topsoil is to ensure that there is fertile ground all the way down to the core. If our ground is good in its depth, we never have to worry about what will be on the surface.

If we don't have a principle in our core, there is no way we can ever be consistent as we navigate through life.

People are like that back yard. They spend a great amount of time cultivating the grass that other people can see but avoid digging up the trash that is buried. For them, it is about the beauty of the grass, not the quality of the dirt.

The trash in our lives can exist for a variety of reasons. You may have toxic contamination in your core that is passed down from your parents. I've never heard of the perfect parents, but some are definitely worse than others. Some parents have so much toxic waste in their own core that they pass it directly to their children. This could be through abuse, neglect, abandonment, or even criticism and judgment. If a parent doesn't feel good about himself or herself, it is difficult to impossible to love a child unconditionally.

If you have the situation where either of your parents were critical, demanding, or emotionally unavailable, those interactions have made their way down into your identity as a person. Please understand, however, this self-concept is not real. Your value is not decided by the words or actions of a hurting person, even if that person is your father.

Our toxic waste also comes from personal negative experiences. If you struggled in school or in sports, those situations can lead to a conclusion of low worth. You could wrongly conclude that you don't have value because you have failed at things you see as important. This is what I did with my dyslexia.

When people have a failure or multiple failures in their lives, they often conclude that they are "a failure." Their results from certain behaviors become a self-imposed identity. A person who has attempted several businesses, but failed each time will likely come to the conclusion that he/she is not cut out to be a businessperson. You are not a failure just because you struggled in an area or tried many times but never succeed. It doesn't matter how many times a boxer gets knocked to the ground as long as he continues gets up. Those feelings of being knocked down in your memory do not need to define you. They are events, results of particular thinking and behavior patterns in your life. Your failures are not representation of your potential. You get the opportunity to define yourself. You must be careful of how you label yourself because those labels contribute to that buried toxic waste.

Some of your toxic self-image comes from poor decisions you have made in your life. Every decision we make is connected to a consequence. If we choose to do the wrong things, that decision will come with a price. You might look back over your life and see a pattern of bad decisions. You may have struggled in choosing good relationships, or careers, or making good financial decisions. Bad decisions lead to bad results. How you see yourself is largely based on how you see the results in your life. When you evaluate your results as "poor," that adds to your buried toxic waste.

Sometimes, however, that toxicity is buried in our back yard, and we lack awareness. A woman, for example, might not know that she seeks attention from emotionally damaged men. She may just go through her life with a train-wreck pattern of relationships. Most of the time, the contamination of our core is not intentional. Sometimes, we don't even know that such contamination exists because we don't see it with objectivity.

It is much more work to dig down into the crevices of our core and face things we'd hoped would simply fade away. Honestly, most people focus more on the surface areas of their lives because it is easier and gives more immediate results. We all want the beautiful lawn, and there is nothing wrong with that. It is just important to recognize that if you want the beauty of your surface to last, you must create the foundation of character.

Character is the level of transparency between what is in our core and what we show on the surface. Usually when we refer to character it is based in good principles. Just because someone is toxic in their core and toxic in their presentation, does not mean that that person has character. He might be consistent and even transparent, which is admirable, but his transparency is based on things we don't tend to value. If someone is a thief and openly admits it, we don't say, "Oh, that person has character." When we speak of someone who has good character, we typically use solid principles as the cornerstone for that evaluation.

For example, not only is the principle of "honesty" one of the Ten Commandments, it is a positive principle that a high majority of the world population, regardless of religion, sees as admirable. Most people value the principle of honesty, yet many do not necessarily have the character of honesty. They are honest when they feel the need to be honest. They are honest when they know they have to be honest or when they know someone is watching. Their honesty might be based on context or situation. Being dishonest is not a big deal as long as they don't believe it hurts anybody or if the end results justify it. These people's honesty is the manicured lawn that that only goes a few inches deep. They believe they manage their honesty in such a way that others will believe they are an honest person.

Having the character of honesty, however, is not as easy as having a presentation of honesty. Anybody can be honest when they feel like it. But being honest only when it benefits us will never build respect in others.

If you want to have the character of honesty, you will have to choose to be honest all the way down to your core. This means that you have to be honest even when it doesn't benefit you. It means that you have to be honest even if nobody is looking. It means you have to be honest even when it is inconvenient. It means that you have to be honest, not only regarding the big things, but also with the little things. It means that you have to be honest, even if it costs you. When you are an honest person to this depth, you will be amazed how people gravitate to you with trust.

I remember working with a man who was an avid hunter. One day we were talking about some of his hunting experiences. I'm not a hunter, and he was explaining some of the rules to me. He said that there was a piece of private land they like to hunt on that doesn't have adequate postings. I questioned what he meant. He said that the law requires a landowner to post "No Hunting" signs every couple of hundred feet. He said that on this piece of private property, the owner has part of his property line posted, but there is a stretch where there are no signs for over one thousand feet. He said, "Because he doesn't have it posted properly there, that is where we cross." My question to this man was,

"But you know that he doesn't want people hunting on his property because you saw the other signs." This man looked at me like I was crazy and said, "It's his own fault if people hunt his property because he doesn't post his property based on what the law states." I dropped the issue and moved on because I realized that this man was not making his decisions based on core principles. This guy was negotiating what he determined to be "the right thing" based on what he wanted to do. When I witnessed his rationalization, he lost my respect because I knew that he would only be honest if he had to.

Following valued principles cannot be based on what we feel like doing at the time. If we change our surface presentation to match our environment, we are not living a principle driven life, we are acting like a chameleon. When other people see us change our spots based on the situation we are in, they start to not trust us. In order to build trust, we must be consistent in what we do and say.

When other people see us change our spots based on the situation we are in, they start to not trust us.

The only way to never contradict yourself is to always speak from the character at your core. Some people are good liars, but they eventually always back themselves into a corner with their own words. Every lie a person tells requires an average of 12 lies to support the original lie. For each of those 12 lies, it takes another 12 lies. You can really see how the number of lies can grow exponentially. I don't know about most people, but I can't keep 144 pieces of information straight. The only way to be consistent with 144 statements is to make sure they are all based on the same core of truth. If you know you responded to a situation based on a core value, you won't have to think about what you said.

Have you ever heard the saying that you can't judge a book by its cover? This is absolutely true. I have walked through the video store many times trying to find an interesting movie to rent for the evening. On several occasions I have picked up a movie box that looked very interesting. Laura and I tend to like martial arts action films. We will look at the pictures on the movie box and see guys

performing flying kicks and super stunts. So we rent the
unknown movie with great anticipation, only to find out that
the entire movie budget was given to the outside of the box.
The box was high budget, but the movie was low budget.

Don't be like that movie—all box and no content. Your
true value is not going to be found by others in your outward
presentation. It is found in the substance of your character.
What good is a fancy lawn if it is not stable? Things might not
be as pretty for a while once you start focusing your attention
into the core, but the process will pay you in the long run.
When you are the same on the outside as you are on the
inside, you are strong and you will finally be able to reach
your potential.

Great blessings and great stresses reveal true character

It is important to know how to recognize true character in
us and in others. I find that people tend to see what they want
to see, instead of seeing signs of poor character. They
rationalize away indicators of poor character as being
situational or an isolated event. Many times, those isolated
events aren't isolated at all; they are simply revealing the true
core coming to the surface. The way that we evaluate a
person's true character is to see them under great blessings
or great stresses.

People often believe that wealth, fame, power, and
influence corrupt individuals. The truth of the matter is these
things don't corrupt people, they reveal people. If somebody
has poor character, such as delusions of superiority or
selfishness, this deficit is somewhat hidden when they don't
have the position to be superior or the power to control
anybody. If this person obtains promotion, authority, and
power, the existing poor character is given a channel to come
to the surface. With the resources at hand, they might use
their money or position to get what they want at the expense
of someone else. The tendency for selfishness was always

there for this individual—the blessings of wealth or power didn't cause it.

Never shy away from the accomplishments in your life that might bring you wealth or influence. These results are not inherently bad. In fact, they are good if they are built on solid character. Focus on developing your character so strongly that when you receive great blessings, you will manage them effectively and, in turn, be a blessing to others.

I have heard many people make negative comments about wealth. They say things like, "I would never want to be wealthy because I don't value materialism." This comment seems to come from a humble and grounded person. Most of the time, however, a negative comment towards money is based in false humility. Being critical of materialism is a good way to hide behind the real issue because there are examples of materialism all around us all the time. The sheer existence of credit cards is an example of people being backwards regarding their view of money.

When somebody says they wouldn't want to be wealthy, it means something different than it sounds. Such a statement is more likely to be made from a position of fear or insecurity. This person is saying that they don't believe they are capable of making great fortune, or that they don't trust themselves if they were to make it.

Simply put, wealth doesn't cause materialism, a focus on material things as a way to feel good about ourselves causes materialism. The truth is that many individuals, who actually have wealth because they applied principles to obtain it, don't tend to feel the need to show or flaunt it. It is usually the people who are wealth wannabes, who try and prove to everybody that they are rich.

Money, power, authority, fame, and influence are nothing more than magnifiers of character. If you wanted to see what a person is truly like at their core, put $10,000,000 in their bank account, and put their picture on the cover of People Magazine. Whatever they are on the inside will come bubbling up to the surface fairly quickly. If someone has great character and a serving heart, they will use that money for good. They could give $1,000,000 per year to charity and have the free time to travel and meet the needs of the world. This is why even the most noble and humble of persons would never wish to avoid wealth.

If someone has poor character, however, they would probably take the same $10,000,000 and focus only on themselves, even at the cost of harming others. Money has no character of its own—it only reflects that of its user.

Likewise, <u>stress and conflict will reveal character</u>. People are like teabags—their true flavor comes out in hot water.

Money has no character of its own—it only reflects that of its user.

When everything is going well in a person's life, he can manage his attitudes and behaviors quite effectively. Most people know the right answers to what living correctly should look like. Anybody can present the way he needs to for a short time. Under stress and conflict, however, his ability to maintain a proper image decreases. As his mask drops, what is in his core tends to come out.

Andy was a nice guy according to all those around him. His life was pretty mellow and easy. He looked good, smelled good, and seemed to be in control with everything in his life. Andy was successful in business and a natural athlete. In both arenas he could usually win on talent. But, when Andy was not winning, things changed. A side of Andy came out that was not pretty. Andy became ruthless and had no regard for the safety of the other players. He broke the rules and became belligerent when he was called on it. Everything came down to the win for Andy—a win at all costs. Andy was a horrible loser and pouted with irritability for the rest of the day after a loss. The next game, however, he showed up with a big smile on his face and acted like nothing ever happened.

So, how does one understand what was going on with Andy? Was he a guy with great character who just didn't handle losing well? Did he have a split personality? Or, was he simply overly competitive?

No, it is a character issue. Andy was only able to tolerate himself if he was on top. Because he was talented, he was usually on top. Thus, his superficial identity was rarely threatened and he appeared calm and in control, but his character was still not based in anything solid. So, Andy couldn't stand to lose because losing in a game made him feel like a loser in life. He would not tolerate being a loser in life, so he did anything to win. But, one cannot feel truly strong and secure when they don't feel secure under their surface. Therefore, Andy's behavior kept him living his life with nothing more than a *mask* of success.

The thing about character is that it is consistent through contexts. Thus, if we understand what someone's character is like beneath their outward appearance, it is predictable how they will act in all areas of their life. In Andy's case, one could predict that he would show the same dirty fighting techniques in business or his relationships if he ever got to the point of feeling like he was losing. In fact, that is exactly what happened. Andy got married to a sweet gal who was enamored with his presence of confidence. Their marriage went along well for a few years because she simply did everything Andy wanted and it made him feel like he was winning. However, when some problems started to surface in their relationship and Andy started to feel criticism, he started to not fight fair. He used control and manipulation to keep his wife in place. He told his wife that she was crazy and immature and convinced her that their problems where her fault. Andy spoke with such confidence that his wife accepted his logic for several years. When they finally divorced, Andy became vengeful towards her, telling everybody that she was the problem behind their breakup and alienated her from their friendships. He really hit her below the belt.

One might ask, "Where did that come from, that wasn't Andy." But honestly, it was. That poor character was there all along. It showed itself before he got married. When people saw it on the football field, they just didn't know that they were looking at character. People easily dismissed Andy's negative behavior as competitiveness, when in reality they should have seen it as Andy's true flavor.

You will shape your character when you have either great blessings or great stresses. If you don't like your attitude when you are under stress, you cannot explain it away as the stress talking. That stress is simply revealing to you the things that might be hidden in your core. Don't dismiss them. If you don't face those pieces of ugliness, they will continue to control you. As painful as it might be to face things about ourselves that are negative, it is much more painful to live life with a mask that will hold us back from achieving what we desire in our hearts. It is better to recognize that you have some toxic waste in your backyard than attempt to convince yourself that your grass is healthy, only to have it constantly dying.

If anything external changes your situation, nothing really changes within you.

Never wish that a windfall would come to change your situation. It is very tempting to desire a quick fix for our troubles. Even if you had a windfall, your character needs to be strong enough to benefit from it. Many people, who file for bankruptcy to remove their debt, never change their spending habits and find themselves in a similar situation a few years down the road. If anything external of you changes your situation, nothing really changes.

Once you understand the way to identify problems in character, you are on your way to growth. You are going to feel the most successful when you are growing because you will be reaching for the greatness of your potential.

To be successful, you must train your character

A man once asked me, "Ok, I want to be seen as a person of character. But how do I develop character in my own life?" The way we form character is by doing the right things when we think that the right things seem small or unimportant. People tend to focus on big things in their life and believe that small things don't matter. We need to not rationalize the small decisions as being small. We deal with many more "small" things on a daily basis. We can use our reasoning for why these things don't matter, but when we do that, we fail to develop the consistency of principle decisions all the way down to our core. We might think, "Stores make a lot of money, it was their fault they had the wrong price tag on that item." Keep in mind; if we allow ourselves to rationalize the small things, it is not that big of leap to rationalize the big things. If we are willing to cheat somebody out of one dollar, we could find a justification to cheat somebody out of a million dollars.

Character is formed when you walk back into the store after you were given too much change. Character is formed when you stand up and accept responsibility when nobody would ever know you did something wrong. Good character is developed when you choose not to sue a restaurant because you burnt yourself on coffee. True character is crafted when you show love to people who don't seem to deserve it. Sharp character is crafted when you choose to pay the real, but higher, price for something, even though it was mismarked. Strong character is opening the door for somebody, even though they will be ahead of you in line. Solid character is formed when you decide to play by the rules, regardless if the other team doesn't—even if it means losing the game.

You will not define your character when you feel good about it. It is not difficult to do the right thing when everything is in your favor. People don't tend to cheat after they have the lead in the game. It is easy to play by the rules when victory is on our side. <u>Your character is developed</u> <u>during the times you make quality decisions in the middle of</u> <u>your life falling apart</u>. When the right decision hurts, you will know that you are crafting something great in yourself.

You see, people are like iron ore—they seem strong, yet they are filled with impurities that weaken them. Adversity in life is like the blacksmith's fire and the anvil. The process of adversity has the power to remove our weak components and leave the strength of steel. When you temper yourself through the fires of life and make quality, character based decisions, you remove the impurities of weakness out of your character. It takes a great deal of heat and pounding to shape iron ore into steel that is strong. But raw iron is not strong enough to survive the demands of stress. Iron will break and crumble when it is put to the test. But steel that has been tempered by fire and shaped with a hammer will stand strong and not break. What form of metal would you rather be?

The process of adversity has the power to remove our weak components and leave the strength of steel.

The more you work on developing strong, character-based decisions, the more likely you will make good solid decisions when you are under stress. In many ways, you will be developing "character memory," much like how we develop muscle memory by practicing the correct movements in sports. Professional athletes practice the basics over and over again to get their muscles to do the right things without having to think it through.

I was speaking with Shihan (master instructor) Rick, who is a fifth degree black belt in Aikido and holds a total of 5 different black belts in different martial arts. Shihan Rick stated, "Anybody can learn the necessary techniques to test for a black belt in a matter of a few weeks. But techniques are not enough to have the skill of a black belt. The muscles need to develop the memory of doing the right moves at the right time in order to be effective in real life. If one ever needed to use a martial art to defend themselves, it is not going to be in a controlled setting where the attacker tells you what he is going do." He was saying that a person on the street is not going to say, "I'm going to punch you in the stomach with my right hand now."

Shihan Rick teaches that in order to do the right things, you need to practice the right things, again and again, until your brain doesn't need to think about what the right things are. This process takes years of consistent practice—going over the same moves thousands of times. You don't just practice when you feel like you need to. You discipline your muscles even when your muscles hurt. After you have trained your muscles to do the right things, your body will lead you to be successful when you are not expecting it.

Character is the same principle for your decisions. If you constantly train your character to align with principles, you will eventually act successfully without having to think through every situation. Have you ever noticed how some people just consistently have good things happen in their lives? Well, that is not luck. Those good things are the accumulation of quality decisions that that person has made consistently over years of discipline. Remember, overnight success usually takes about five years.

Once you train your character to help you make good decisions in your life, making the right decisions in the right times will allow you to reach much greater heights of success in your own life.

Probably the best thing about living your life with principle is that it is actually easier. Imagine if you had to think through every situation that came your way as unique. That would be like trying to learn how to drive a car all over again if you turned down an unfamiliar street. But that is not how it works. Once you learn the principles of driving a car, those same fundamentals will apply in 99 percent of situations you encounter. Likewise, once you understand the underlying principles that apply in your life, the right answers become simple answers. As you use principles as the

cornerstone for how to live your life, you develop solid
character. Once you have solid character, that character will
help you make good decisions and lead you to your greater
potential.

Life is an ongoing battle. You will have to be ready to
withstand what is coming at you. I would imagine that if you
were a sword and entering battle, you would likely want to be
the type of sword that had been strengthened to withstand
impact. Every time you face and overcome adversity in your
life, that fire tempers your strength. Remember, swords were
not designed for show—they were designed for a purpose.
They were designed to achieve victory. So are you. Cutting
corners on your own forging process to spend more time on
the polishing process will not help you when you have to fight
for what you want. Weak but pretty swords don't serve a
purpose, other than decoration on a shelf. Your life has a
much greater potential than being superficial and pretty.
Your life has a purpose, and that purpose comes with a fight.

Take Away Discussion Questions

1. What are your thoughts about how the emperor chose to evaluate character?

2. Why do you think many people never dig down to face issues in their character?

3. How has a hidden or ignored issue in your life bubbled up to the surface when you least expected it?

4. Have you ever been on a used car lot and the salesman came out to greet you? In this situation, did you ever feel that what he was saying just wasn't quite right? What do you think you were experiencing?

5. When people only focus on learning the outward techniques to be successful, they rarely ever get the results they seek. Why is this?

6. True success requires transparency. What does this mean to you?

7. The fire of adversity reveals character. What are some examples where this has proven true in your experience?

8. Setting your sights on something great in your life will expose your weaknesses. Will you come to a decision to face those issues and pursue your dreams, or hide from those things and never grow?

9. Have you ever wished that you had wealth or fame in the hopes of avoiding some of your challenges? What are your thoughts about how wealth, power, fame, and popularity only magnify character flaws?

10. What are some of the ways you can envision training your character to be inline with your goals?

11. What is the one thing you are going to take away from this chapter and put into practice in your life, starting now?

Chapter 4

You Will See It When You Believe It
The Principle of Vision

> *The most pathetic person in the world is someone*
> *who has sight, but has no vision.*
>
> — *Helen Keller*

As he gazed into the vastness of the landscape, his heart began to pound as he realized what he was about to do. He stepped off the ladder and his foot settled softly into the fine dust. The small cloud of powder he produced seemed to linger as if time stood still. He never felt so light, and for a brief moment he felt he could float away. When he looked over his shoulder he witnessed the magnificent sight of the blue and white planet in the sky. He had just created history. Neil Armstrong was the first man to set foot on the moon. Can you imagine what he might have been feeling knowing what he had just done?

Eight years prior to that step, Neil Armstrong had no idea that his destiny was to go down in history by fulfilling the vision of a dreamer.

It was 1961 when President John F. Kennedy, in a speech given at a joint session of Congress, claimed to the American public that we would land a man on the moon and safely return him to earth before the end of the 1960's. At the time President Kennedy cast this vision, the world didn't have the technological foundation to support it. Right before President Kennedy raised this challenge, the United States had just accomplished sending Alan Shepard Jr. on a 15-minute suborbital mission. We were nowhere near being able to travel to the moon and safely return to earth. President Kennedy projected to Congress that such a daunting task would likely cost nine billion dollars.

At the time of this speech, the United States was not leading in the space race. The Soviet Union was the first to send their Sputnik satellite into space in 1957 and they also beat the United States by having Yuri Gagarin become the first man in space. There were likely many experts within the United States who thought that President Kennedy was speaking foolishly and should have waited until the science was available to support such an outlandish claim. There were others who believed that President Kennedy's statements were not sincere, but only a ploy to win the cold war with the Soviets.

John F. Kennedy was killed on November 22, 1963, but the vision he cast two years earlier had already been put into motion. The Apollo moon project was a huge vision that took many years, cost many lives and over twenty-five billion dollars. President Kennedy's vision came to reality on July 20, 1969, when Apollo 11 commander, Neil Armstrong stepped out of the Lunar Module and onto the surface of the moon. The American public listened in awe to his immortal words "That's one small step for man; one giant leap for mankind."

After NASA accomplished the goal President Kennedy cast almost ten years earlier, nobody thought Kennedy was foolish. He was considered a visionary.

Your dreams are a gift

"I will believe it when I see it." This is a statement we have all heard so many times throughout our life that it is almost accepted as truth. Typically, this statement is uttered after an individual speaks to some form of dream or goal. It could come from a father towards his son who just told him that he was going to get straight "A's" this semester. This type of statement is typically uttered from someone who is promoting skepticism, doubt, and general negativity. Such a person doesn't tend to believe in much and unfortunately sees nothing getting better in his life or the life of others. He will have a negative view of his own personal success, new emerging technologies, personal growth, and even accomplishments on a global scale. He will insist that he is being a realist, but all pessimists consider themselves a "realist."

If you find yourself thinking that you need to see something before you can believe it–stop it! You picked up this book because you want a better life, not to stay in the same place you have always been. Your personal journey of change begins with your ability to see the unseen. To do this, you need to rephrase the above statement to: "I will see it when I believe it."

All pessimists consider themselves a "realist."

Every success in each area of life begins with a dream. I'm not talking about the kind of dreams we have at night. No, when I talk about the dream, I'm talking about a voluntary process of getting your mind to ponder and visualize something that has not yet happened. Being able to see the future you want, regardless of the data in the present.

Martin Luther King stood on the steps of Lincoln Memorial in Washington DC and gave one of the most widely recognized speeches of all time. What is affectionately known as the *I have a dream speech* was given in 1963, yet it is studied by children, whose parents weren't even born at the time it was presented by King. King moved people by casting his vision of harmony between the races. He spoke of concepts, of which in 1963, were radical changes to how society was functioning. This was a huge and impactful dream!

We have all had dreams to some degree. This happens on any level when we allow ourselves to ponder something that we desire in our future. Dreams can be grand, such as influencing an entire nation, or they can be small and personal, such as driving that sports car that we have on our computer screen at work. Maybe you have the dream of getting out of debt and being able to travel the world. Possibly you have the dream of having a good relationship with your spouse or children. Whatever your dreams might be, they are good for you.

Unfortunately, many people take dreaming for granted and they don't place the appropriate value on the gift of the dream.

Human beings are the only creatures known to have the ability to visualize and dream about what is not yet seen. Chimpanzees have been documented to make and use tools naturally in their environment, but these tools tend to be utilized as a direct solution to a problem, such as getting termites out of the ground. Chimps, however, don't seem to have the ability to think abstractly or dream of a better life. That is why human culture has continued to advance in knowledge, whereas chimpanzees have not changed much in the past one hundred years of being observed and evaluated. The gift of the dream seems to be one of the qualities that separate human beings from the rest of the animal kingdom.

The ability to visualize something better in your life will motivate you to move from a stationary position. Your vision combined with a decision to do something about it will lead to action. In order for a person to feel alive, he or she needs to be pursuing something in life. In fact, the Bible states that if a man doesn't have vision he will perish. This is a profound statement. In a sense, if you stop looking forward, you will wither up and rot. That doesn't sound very good! You were not designed to rot, you were designed to grow and achieve in your life.

An ability to dream is special and unique–it is truly a gift from God. In the book of Jeremiah it states, *"For I know the plans I have for you, declares the Lord, plans to prosper you and not to harm you, plans to give you a hope and a future."* You see, God promises you that he will bless your life in ways that are greater than you can think or ask. You might say, "I don't know, I can think and ask pretty big." Yet, sometimes our dreams are just the tip of the iceberg. We think we know what we want and we limit ourselves to that dream. However, once we start the journey and keep that dream in front of us, we may come to discover that our dreams are much bigger than we ever anticipated.

God knows every person better than they know themselves. The dreams he gives to you are not the wrong size. Please understand that a gift from God cannot be returned, it can only be hung out of sight and ignored. Nobody should do that. God has given you a gift when he has given you a dream, what you do with your dreams is your gift back to God.

I remember when I was in high school I wanted to be an Air Force fighter pilot. I had posters of F-15's on my bedroom wall and I put together models of jets. When the movie Top Gun came out, it solidified my dream (even though it was a movie about the Navy). Regardless, I could see myself soaring above the clouds, feeling the speed and raw power of those jet engines under my control. However, I had one stumbling block–my vision. I didn't have 20/20 vision, not even close. This vision issue was an obstacle because in those days you couldn't have corrected vision and be accepted to flight school. So, I dropped the idea of flying F-15's. The dream that was seeded in my youth, however, later took me down a road that led to a college education and then focused my attention towards a residency in psychology with the Air Force.

In the Air Force I worked with pilots and got the
opportunity to fly (as a passenger). The Air Force led me to
Idaho and to a positive career and association. So in a sense,
where I am today has roots from a dream and posters on my
wall from high school. One could say that I had to give up on
the dream of flying, but really I traded that dream for much
bigger ones. From being a psychologist in the Air Force, I saw
the demand that was placed on fighter pilots. Many suffered
in their marriages and family relationships. They were
deployed frequently and had to move bases every few years.
Knowing what I know now, if I had to choose between being a
fighter pilot and being a psychologist, I would pick the same
path that led me to where I am at today.

Because I had the dream of flying jets, this led me
through doors that I might not have even seen. I didn't even
know how to think or ask for what I needed out of life when I
was staring up at those posters in my youth. But God knows
what we need and can provide the direction if we are willing
to provide the propulsion.

Many people believe that they must know exactly what
they are going to do before they start pursuing anything.
Pursuing dreams does not work like that, as clearly evidenced
in my own story. Think of life options or choices as doors off
a long hallway. Some people stand at one end of this hall in
an emotionally paralyzed state because they don't know what
door to pick. They try to evaluate all the doors from their
limited vantage point and make "the right" decision.
Unfortunately, this strategy does not work well.

If a person sets her sights on a dream or goal and begins
to pursue it, she will be starting to walk down the hall. This
process leads her past many doors, some of which she didn't
even know existed. In the pursuit of her dreams, she might
find herself walking past a door that captures her attention
and she decides to enter and begin a new journey. This
process couldn't have happened, however, if she had not
been moving towards her initial dreams in the first place.
This has happened to me many times during my life,

including how I got to the point of writing this book. I can't tell you how many times I've uttered the words "I'll never", only to find myself doing that very thing later through a series of choices of following dreams.

The truth is, every ounce of forward progress hinges on a dream or vision. So why do we give up on something that occurs so naturally in our youth. It clearly is not more productive or functional to give up on dreams. We may pass it off as being more matured, logical, or reasonable, but that really isn't it. I believe that people give up dreaming because they don't want to be disappointed if their dreams aren't realized. People have fear of failure and they doubt that they have the ability to change the course of their lives.

> *Every ounce of forward progress hinges on a dream or vision.*

This level of fear doesn't bind kids in the same way. It is like my youngest son, Logan, learning to ski. Logan just points his skis down the mountain and goes for it. Adults think too much about what might go wrong. They think about falling, using the proper technique, or how they look to others. Their fear hinders their process.

If you want to be around big dreamers, simply surround yourself with children. I have three boys, all of whom have huge dreams. My oldest son, Dakota, somehow became passionately interested in sharks. He reads everything he can get about sharks and it is typically a given that he is the most knowledgeable person about sharks in any given group of people, even though at this time he is only fourteen years old. A couple years ago we sent him to a marine biology camp at Sea World. Due to his passion with sharks, he was able to teach some of the camp counselors things they didn't know. When Dakota starts spinning his dream for what he is going to accomplish in his life with marine biology, we listen in awe. He talks about making a fortune in discovering a new species of shark, developing new technologies to study sharks, and even having a home with a shark tank built into a wall in his bedroom. Dakota's younger brother, Hunter, is going to be an inventor. He is constantly sharing his ideas about possible inventions, such as hovercrafts and transporters. When Dakota and Hunter start bouncing ideas off of each other, their dreams get bigger and bigger. There doesn't seem to be any limitation to their dreams, such as technology or physics. They simply dream.

Kids are like this, aren't they? Kids in grade school and junior high talk about being rock stars, wealthy businessmen, actresses, novelists, and curing disease. They talk about having huge houses, lots of land, fleets of cars, and traveling the world. By the time kids get into high school, their dreams tend to be bound more to the "reality" of their grades, talents, potential for college, and established careers promoted by guidance counselors. By the time those kids graduate high school and enter adulthood, many of them have placed significant limitations on what they can achieve. They begin, unfortunately, to live a life of least resistance, instead of pushing themselves to greatness. Benjamin Franklin said, "Many people die at twenty-five and aren't buried until they are seventy-five." Benjamin Franklin was referring to people giving up on their own visions and dreams.

When a person embraces the gift of the dream, it pleases the giver. How would you like it if you invested your time and heart into making a gift for your close friend, only to have her not even take it out of the box? What if she said, "Oh, I'm not good enough to have this. It is too nice for someone like me." How would that make you feel? Would you think "Wow that must be a really special gift, I'm glad I gave it to her." Or, would you see it as a wasted gift? That gift could have been something that changed her life for the better, but now she will never know what could have been. I would imagine that if someone treated your gift this way, you would have wished that you gave that gift to someone else.

Your ability to dream is a gift and so is the ability to bring your dreams into reality. Many people get the gift of a dream, but choose to not unwrap it because they feel scared or unworthy. These individuals are only hurting themselves by leaving their dreams in the box. It might not be packaged exactly like you want, but it will still be a reality as long as you don't give up. God gave you the gift of the ability to dream, what you do with your dream is your gift back to God.

Dreams are not limited by facts

Ben and Janet is a couple who has been married twenty-five years and has three children. They came to counseling after years of feeling like roommates living in the same home. Janet complained that she was the peacekeeper in the home and was the glue that held the family together. She became increasingly frustrated with Ben when he seemed to spend all his energy either at work, out with his friends, or doing his own "selfish things." Janet collected more and more data in their marriage about how Ben was self-centered and would never change. The challenges in their marriage came to a head and Janet finally disclosed that she was willing to divorce Ben. This statement hit Ben like a ton of bricks and he decided that he was willing to do whatever it took to save the relationship. They entered counseling and Janet's complaints quickly became evident.

Ben was self-centered, unemotional, bull-headed, and was used to getting what he wanted. But, after his marriage was falling apart right before his eyes, he became willing to face his challenges, listen to counsel, and change. Ben believed that he could change and their marriage could be restored. Janet, on the other hand, struggled with seeing the possibility of change. She came to counseling, but each session was focused on how Ben would never change. Even though Ben was doing many things correctly, Janet interpreted his actions as being "temporary." She wouldn't give Ben any credit for his efforts and kept returning to how many times she was hurt by his behavior in the past. Session after session they came in talking about the same things. There was no forward progress in their marriage, mostly because Janet didn't believe there could be. Many of our sessions focused on what Janet wanted. She would say that she wanted a loving, trusting, relationship with a man who thinks of her before himself. I then turned it to her and informed her how important it was to believe that dream was possible.

Janet started to intellectually understand how important the vision of success is. She, like most people, struggled to get information that she intellectually understood to move into her heart where she could believe it. The longest journey a person can take is the twelve inches between their head and their heart. People understand things much more easily than they accept and believe things. And this journey took some time for Janet because she did not want to set herself up for failure or disappointment. Although this is understandable, if she didn't allow herself to take the risk, she was inevitably locking herself into certain failure.

A vision of a good marriage started working itself into Janet's heart. She started to soften her hardened exterior and began communicating to Ben how she appreciated the way he was sincerely trying to do better. It was also very good on Ben's part to not give up doing the right things when Janet was struggling with her belief. His consistency in following counsel during her challenges was essential for her to turn around. As Janet opened up her heart to the risk of the dream of a happy marriage, their progress in counseling took off. They became like sponges, soaking up what they needed to be doing for each other. They created a positive momentum in their relationship and within a couple months they no longer needed to come in for counseling. I wish that every couple I meet with would have these kinds of results

There is a certain level of comfort that comes with familiarity. Many people would rather live in the muck of life, as long as it is familiar, rather than venture into unfamiliar territory, even if it is better ground. They would rather aim for nothing and hit it, than aim at something and possibly miss.

You might be saying, "But I have set goals before in my
life, only to give up and feel more disappointed. I'm not sure
goals work."

It is important to understand that there is a difference
between goals and dreams. Goals are great, but they tend to
be quite specific and sometimes lack an emotional
connection. A goal can be hit or missed, but a dream lives on.
Goals connected to dreams form a powerful relationship.

You might say, "I have a goal to lose twenty pounds; what
is wrong with that?"

Good for you. There is nothing wrong with setting a goal.
A person who sets such a goal will be more likely to
accomplish it versus someone who never takes that step. But
the problem with only keeping it at the goal level is that goals
can be easily abandoned. We might want to lose a certain
amount of weight, but when we are in the moment of
desiring the big piece of cake that is placed in front of us, a
goal specific to only weight can go out the window. If it is only
about us, we will easily let it go.

A vision or a dream will have an emotional component to
it. If we allow ourselves to really dream big, the emotion of
that process will bring about an excitement and sense of
expectancy we possibly haven't felt since our youth.

Many times, it takes faith in something
greater than us to see beyond our current *Dreams are*
situation. Most people simply evaluate *not limited to*
their past, calculate the data, and then *the facts.*
predict their future. Thus, if they had
failed several times when they stretched themselves, they will
draw the faulty conclusion that they would only fail again if
they try again. In a sense, they develop a learned helplessness.
They believe, "No matter what I do I will not succeed." At this
point, it is easy to give up trying. The definition of faith,
however, states that we believe in something even when there
is an absence of evidence to support such beliefs.

You will only realize a dream in your life if you stretch
beyond the existing data. Dreams are not limited to the facts.

If this were true, Janet and Ben would have never grown in their relationship. If their future was the same as their past, they would currently be miserable. They achieved because they chose to believe based on what they wanted, not what they had. You too can visualize for more in your life. Don't get caught up in the data, focus on the dream.

The how comes after the dream

A woman named Carol I once spoke with expressed the same fear that most people have. Carol said, "If I allow myself to believe that my life could be better and it doesn't happen, I will be disappointed and feel like a greater failure. How is setting goals going to change things, what would I do differently?" Carol was feeling stressed out because she was in her fifties and feeling insecure in her job and financial future. She felt stuck, with no options to change her situation.

When I suggested to Carol that she needed to start by believing that she could change her situation, she responded with the most common question, "How?"

Carol's question is an ongoing dilemma that most people face. Before they allow themselves to dream for something greater in their lives, they want to know how it will happen. They believe that once they see the path, and that path makes sense, then they can start setting goals for the results down that path.

The problem is, the how always comes after the dream. If we attempt to get the how first, it simply won't work because we aren't even open to it. How are you going to recognize a path if you don't believe a destination exists? The dream must come first. Once you believe that something can be better in your life, you will become open to the paths when they present themselves. In fact, when you believe in your dreams, you will attract the procedure or the vehicle to achieve them. If you don't believe that opportunity will ever visit you, when it knocks at your door you will dismiss it as only the wind.

Thomas Edison continues to hold the record for the number of patents. He was a prolific inventor. In order to invent and create, someone must see the results in their mind's eye, before they start the process of how they will accomplish the goal. Thomas Edison saw the success of his many inventions long before the physical manifestation of them came into reality. Could you imagine what would have happened if Thomas Edison waited to start developing the light bulb until he knew exactly the steps that would be required? Well, he wouldn't have done it.

It is sometimes quite difficult to embrace a dream for something new and great in our lives when it feels like that could never happen. As I was stressing this point to Carol, she said, "That sounds like motivational speaker stuff. I have heard those kinds of messages throughout my life." As she was trying to point out why that information didn't work for her, she said, "It would be easy for those motivational speakers to have a positive attitude, they make millions of dollars talking about it. If I made millions of dollars, I could have a positive attitude as well."

The problem is, Carol got the order of events wrong. People who coach on success principles don't stumble on millions of dollars then get inspired to talk about positive mental attitude once they have the money. I have never heard of someone who won the lottery and then started a success lecture series. People who teach concepts, such as the power of dreams and vision, teach from their own experience. They apply the principles of dreaming for more when they have little, or even nothing. Such experts do not promote dreams because they have success—they have success because they promote their own dreams.

Accomplished people do not promote dreams because they have success—they have success because they promote their own dreams.

So how do we decide to take the risk of beginning to dream before we have the security of knowing how that dream will be realized? Opening yourself up to the possibility of something better in life is a vulnerable experience. It hurts to hope for more and be let down. Yet, your risk of not dreaming will be a greater cost.

Think of it this way, if a person had a 20 percent chance of something positive happening or a 0 percent chance, which one of those options should they choose? Clearly, you would urge them to choose 20 percent. What if this person only had a 10 percent chance? Wouldn't it still be smarter to opt for the possibility of something rather than settle for nothing? Why would anybody not even give themselves a chance to shoot for something they want? Yet this is just what people do. They choose "nothing" instead of a chance at something, because they don't see the chance of change, or achievement, or growth as being probable.

God gives you the gift of a dream and places the crossroads in your life to accomplish it. It says in Ecclesiastes "time and chance come together for every person." That means that you don't need to worry about how your dreams will be realized–once you begin believing in your dreams, God will give you the mechanism to achieve them. You will run into the right people, read the right things, be in the right places, and the right ideas will invade your thoughts when you least expect it. Once you open yourself up to understand that God's gift of the dream is bigger than you, you can start approaching each day with an attitude of faith and expectancy. This allows God to do his part and bring your dreams into reality.

Take Away Discussion Questions

1. Are there areas in your life where you are not allowing yourself to dream? What reasons do you focus on to justify this?

2. Many people choose a predictable, safe, and unchanging life. Why do you think people opt for this path?

3. What great dreams could be possibly in your future?

4. Your dreams are a gift from God and what you do with them is your gift back to God. How have you demonstrated or failed to demonstrate this in your life?

5. One definition of hell is a place where you can view the life you led and also view the potential life you could have had if you only would have followed your dreams. What regret might you experience if you don't follow your dreams?

6. If God gives you a dream, you will learn something from it. Your lesson will either be in the form of self-discipline or regret. What does this statement mean to you?

7. Your dreams are not limited by facts. Most every large and worthwhile dream was once thought to be impossible based on the existing facts at the time. What "facts" do you tend to focus on?

8. Many people mistakenly believe that they must know the path to their dreams before they allow themselves to embrace the dream. Have you ever found yourself falling into this trap? What happened?

9. Since most people in life are so afraid to dream because of the possibility of being let down, they find it easier to steal the dreams of others than to risk dreaming again themselves. Have you ever experienced this? How did someone steal your dream?

10. When others are negative about your dreams, they often have good intentions. What might those be?

11. It is important to seek a positive association of people who will help build up your dreams. Who would be some people who could help cultivate your dreams?

12. What is the one thing you are going to take away from this chapter and put into practice in your life, starting now?

Chapter 5

You Will Not Drift to Success
The Principle of Purposefulness

Always bear in mind that your own resolution to
succeed, is more important than any other one thing

— *Abraham Lincoln*

The sun started to show itself by shining across the
crashing waves and clearing the traces of fog, which had
settled in during the night. The morning air was cool and the
dampness from the prior night's rain still lingered. Regan
and his wife of seventeen years had a Saturday morning ritual.
They got up before their children stirred, when the morning
was quiet and still. Cheryl made a pot of strong coffee while
Regan toasted each of them a bagel and spread the cream
cheese. They slipped into their jackets and made their way
out onto their deck. They had a favorite sitting spot, where
they could drink their coffee while taking in the view of the
Puget Sound. They loved everything about the water–the
soothing sounds, the rhythm of the waves, and the great
variety boats carving their individual paths through the water.
Regan and Cheryl had looked out over that view for many
years, watching in awe all the people navigating the majestic
boats. Regan loved all the different kinds of boats, but he,
along with Cheryl were particularly drawn to the sailboats.
There was something about how sailboats seemed to be in

harmony with the sea. The sailboats reminded Regan of the peacefulness he felt on those early Saturday mornings before his busy life took over.

Regan visualized himself on their own boat, cutting through the wind and the waves. He and Cheryl talked at length about the dream of getting a boat "someday" and cruising up and down the Sound in front of their own house and pulling into quaint little harbors in Washington. There was always, however, a reason why they needed to wait until a better time to get a boat, yet they continued to talk about the future. Regan's dream eventually developed and expanded to the point where he saw himself and Cheryl traveling far beyond their familiar waters and sailing on their own boat to Hawaii.

On this particular Saturday, Regan put his coffee down on the deck railing and said to Cheryl, "I don't think the right time will ever get here, I think we need to get our boat." Cheryl looked over at him as the dew that had collected on the brim of her hood fell onto her cheek,

"Are you sure we can do it?" Cheryl asked with a look of hope in her eyes.

Regan assured her as he gave her a half smile, "We have been talking about doing it for years, I think it is time that we take the leap of faith and pursue it."

That afternoon Regan and Cheryl started looking in the paper for used sailboats. They found a few local boats that were in their price range and they called to arrange viewings. They looked at three different boats that all seemed to need much more work than they wanted to give. When they saw the fourth boat, however, they both knew that they just found their boat. It was a forty-foot boat that was owned by a family who lived out of state. This family only took the boat out about once per year and the boat looked almost new. After a short contemplation Regan and Cheryl made the purchase and became boat owners.

Regan and Cheryl took a very important step in the realization of their dream. It is easy to keep dreams in the "maybe someday" category where it is safe and there is no risk. To realize a dream, there is almost always a leap of faith that is required. This step of commitment, however, is not enough to see the dream to completion. In order for a dream to become reality, one must be purposeful in the pursuit and realization of that dream.

Could you imagine what would happen if Regan and Cheryl took this first step of buying a sailboat, but tried to accomplish their dream without the proper education, experience, and planning? They would never achieve the things they set out to do. Imagine if they took their boat out into the ocean, pointed it to the direction of Hawaii, and waited for their dream to be realized. They would sit, and sit, and sit. Their boat would likely move around, it may even get into a current and travel thousands of miles. But what is the likelihood that this couple would land on the beaches of Hawaii? Almost zero–right? This is because you do not drift to success.

To be successful in the realization of their vision, this couple would have to focus on getting the proper training and experience over a period of time. They would need to take sailing lessons, learn how to tie knots, how to trim sails, how to navigate, and how to follow the rules of the seas. They would have to learn how to read maps, chart courses, and follow proper wind and ocean currents. They would need to learn emergency procedures and how to use their radio. Then, they would need lots of hours on their boat, sailing back and forth in safe waters, just to familiarize themselves with sailing operations. All of these things would take some time. Regan and Cheryl's vision should be cast out for a couple of years to ensure that once they set sail, they are prepared for the journey.

If you are going to have a dream, it is best to prepare yourself to make that dream a reality. If you don't do this, your dreams will haunt you after you have drifted nowhere close to where you want to be. There are things you need to be purposeful about to realize your dreams.

Achieving your goals requires discipline

I guess I like sailing analogies because there are great parallels between navigating a sailboat and making your way through life. This chapter started out with Regan and Cheryl turning their dreams into reality by purchasing their first sailboat. So, lets continue with sailing and the required disciplines to arrive at a desired destination.

I don't know if you have ever been behind the helm of a sailboat. I don't personally own a sailboat, but I spent some time in my youth working and living on a sailboat. During that time I developed a great appreciation and fondness for sailing. What I came to realize was that steering a sailboat is a very different experience than driving a powerboat. In a powerboat, you can set your autopilot for the direction you want to go and the boat follows. This feature does not work well when you are getting your power from the wind.

Sailing requires a great deal of focus and work to get where you want to go. Such is true with your goals.

On a sailboat, if you want to travel directly north, for example, it is very rare that you have wind cooperating by blowing in that same direction. Most of the time in sailing, you are cutting into some percentage of the wind, which causes the boat to tilt, or in sailing terminology "keel." If you want to travel north, you may have to follow a course of northwest, then turn, or "tack" to northeast, creating a type of zigzag movement. As the captain of this ship, not only do you make large shifts in direction, you also will make constant small corrections in heading and sail trim. If you do not constantly attend to these things, you will lose power, sit dead in the water, and potentially drift off course. Sailing requires a great deal of focus and work to get where you want to go. Such is true with your goals.

Some might think that it would be great to set a goal and simply plug in the coordinates, sit back and wait for the results to come flowing in. Life could not be further from this perspective. Achieving goals, like sailing, requires us to continually align our thoughts, words, and actions to our goals. As soon as we get tired and go below deck to take a break, we lose our focus on the things that are required to achieve our goals and we begin to drift.

Unfortunately, most people who have dreams and goals in their life simply drift, hoping to land upon those goals someday. They pull out the dream and review it, they check their current coordinates and even point their boat in the right direction, and then they allow the wind and currents of life to move them. This will never work because being successful in anything is a purposeful event.

Most people have dreams at one point or another in their life, but many do not discipline themselves enough to achieve their potential. Many people don't set goals and therefore don't grow because they choose the path of least resistance. Pursuing goals can seem difficult or even painful to some people. They complain how hard their lives are and then they don't invest the energy to do anything about it. In a sense, they choose what is easier in the moment, but they don't realize that they are not doing themselves any favors. Friends, success in anything in life is only going to be found with proper self-discipline. Since it takes less energy to drift, we must discipline ourselves to not give into what seems to be an easier path.

There are many reasons persons choose to drift through life instead of buckling down and making things happen. One of the reasons people drift is because they simply tolerate where they are. They feel okay with not changing. They might dislike their jobs, but it pays the bills. They might not feel the love they would like in their marriage, but at least they don't fight in front of the kids. They might be overweight, but tell themselves that they enjoy eating their comfort foods too much. They might dream of being financially independent, but they are comfortable with their two incomes from jobs and a couple of nice leased cars parked in the garage. They might feel depressed, but they get up and go to work every day and drag themselves through it. Thus, their lives are acceptable based on minimal standards, which decreases their motivation to change. Do not live your life by such minimal standards.

Thinking of yourself with minimal standards will cause you to become average. Being average doesn't take much effort, but the average marriage doesn't last; the average household income is not enough to pay the bills; the average person is hurting emotionally and is not physically healthy.

You were designed to achieve greatness in your life.

You were not designed to be average. You were designed to be uniquely gifted and special. You were designed to achieve greatness in your life.

We tend to gravitate towards average because it feels normal. It is much easier to stroll with the crowd instead of choosing to run in your own direction. It is easy to be average because we are accepted there. When we don't stand out from others we don't experience resistance. When we don't serve as a threat, we are embraced by the masses. When we are average, we do not serve as a threat to anybody else's lack of progress, so they leave us alone.

When we experience comfort, we often don't have much motivation to change where we are. Even though we might have dreams for more, we rationalize with ourselves that we are "good enough" or "I should be content where I am at."

A comfort zone is a dead zone.

There is nothing wrong with being happy where you are, if you are living your dreams. But most people are not living their dreams—they simply shrink their dreams to match where they are at in their comfort zone. This leads to a long-range feeling of regret.

A comfort zone is a dead zone. A comfort zone has walls that imprison us in such a way that we do not have enough motivation to escape. When we are not stretching towards something great in our lives, we are not growing. If we don't grow, we die–there is no such thing as neutral when it comes to growth.

Like the couple that dreamt of sailing to Hawaii–they could both enjoy their time in Puget Sound while they prepared for their open water voyage, or they could convince themselves that Puget Sound is good enough for them and then settle in to their existing routine. Now, don't get me wrong, the Puget Sound is one of my favorite places. I'm not saying that the Puget Sound is not good enough, but did the couple shrink their dreams to match where they were comfortable? If this is true, they simply robbed themselves of the rewards of achieving a big dream in their lives.

When we settle into our comfort zone, we develop a sense of complacency that strips us of our motivation to act. Even though we have goals and dreams, when we are comfortable we tell ourselves that we have all the time in the world to realize those dreams.

There once was a man who lived in an older home that had a leaky roof. When it was raining outside that water poured in. As this man was placing bowls and cans around the house to catch the drips, he told himself that he needed to get up on the roof and do some repairs. When the rain passed over, however, the drips stopped. When the sun came out and dried up the ground, the man was comfortable in his home and his motivation dropped when it came time for him to go up on the roof and fix the holes. The comfort of a dry house kept him from pushing himself to change things for the stormy weather.

When we act according to our feelings of comfort we tend to drift through life and never achieve the things our hearts desire. It requires self-discipline for us to move towards our goals and dreams when life seems okay in the moment. It takes a purposefulness to step out and accomplish something for our future when the rain is not dripping on our heads.

Another reason people fail to pursue their goals is due to avoiding resistance. People naturally follow the paths of least resistance in life. Most people use naturally occurring forces, such as emotions or public acceptance or approval, to move them because it is easier. It doesn't take any energy, focus, perseverance, or determination. They simply go with the flow, move with the masses, and avoid resistance.

So many people spend their lives trying to avoid the feeling of resistance. They feel that if they have resistance in their lives, they must be doing the wrong things. If their choices aren't popular with their coworkers they must be the wrong choices. If their ideas don't work right away, their ideas must be faulty. If they are struggling with something, they should probably quit. These types of thinking keeps people moving with an apathy that will cause them to never accomplish anything of significance in their lives.

If you don't do things in life that create resistance, you really aren't doing anything different from the masses. Keep in mind, if an airplane doesn't experience resistance it would fall from the sky. The forces that pushes against the plane are what the plane uses fly. You, like the plane, know that you are moving when you feel resistance. If we don't choose to go against the movement of the masses, we will be like lemmings following the next one off the cliff.

The only way to avoid resistance is to drift to where the currents take you.

Anytime you act with purpose in your life you will go against naturally occurring forces. The only way to avoid resistance is to drift to where the currents take you. If we want to sail to Hawaii, we will not have the wind at our backs and the ocean currents in our favor the whole time. We would have to cut into the wind and break through the waves to get where we wish to go. Resistance is just part of the process.

To achieve any worthwhile goal, resistance is not just likely—it is essential. Overcoming resistance is required to shape you into the quality of person necessary to achieve the goals that you seek. If you wish to get stronger in the gym, you cannot simply sit and watch other people work out as a way to achieve your goals. You cannot go to the weights and lift 2 ½

pounds, then expect to receive any benefit from that effort.
In order to accomplish the goal of increased muscle mass,
you need resistance. Your muscles get stronger only when
they have to overcome the adversity of lifting the increasing
weights.

Shortcuts to results with the attempt to bypass resistance
never work. We can't find the perfect spouse, with whom we
never fight. We can't start out at the top of a company so we
never have to deal with a difficult supervisor. Supplements
that we take to bulk up or lose weight never have long-term
results. The reason these things don't work is because we
have to become successful through the process of facing the
resistance and overcoming it. By bypassing resistance, we
don't change. If we don't change, we won't keep any results
we end up with in the short term.

Instead of attempting to avoid resistance, embrace it.
Understand that the burn and sweat that you get when you
work out is the indicator of progress. Understand that the
adversity you face in your relationship with your spouse is
what is going to force the two of you to understand each
other better. The challenges you face in business are there for
a reason–don't look for ways to eliminate them. You will
become stronger, wiser, and better because you pushed
through the resistance in your life.

Finally, people tend to give up on their goals because they
get tired or weary during the journey. When Moses led the
Hebrews out of Egypt, it wasn't long into their journey to the
Promised Land before the masses became disgruntled. They
had been enslaved for generations and slavery was all that
they knew. It wasn't long into their journey when they started
complaining about how hard their life was. They started
talking about "the good ol' days" under Pharaoh's rule. Many
of these Hebrew people started saying things like "At least
under Pharaoh we had a place to sleep and food to eat. It
wasn't that bad."

Many of the Hebrews began to give up on the dream of
freedom and the possibility of living in a land that was

promised to "flow with milk and honey" because they got tired. They became too shortsighted and began focusing too much on their current struggle. Because they got weary, they lost hope and they lost sight of their dream.

It is reported that it is only approximately an 11-day walk across the desert from Egypt to Canaan. Yet, within that time, this mass of people lost their focus on what Moses had communicated to them as God's plan for them. They started developing a negative attitude about the likelihood of their goal. When they got to the outskirts of Canaan, Moses sent twelve spies into the Promised Land to evaluate what they faced.

Ten of the spies came back with reports based in fear. These negative reports fueled the existing doubt the Hebrews already developed during the journey. The masses became weary about what they were supposed to do, thus they did nothing. They would not move forward and overcome the adversity that they faced to achieve their goal. Because they didn't push forward toward the dream that God gave them, they ended up walking in circles in the desert for forty years. God waited until that entire generation died off before he gave the Hebrews another shot at the dream.

When we give up because we are tired or weary, we typically don't fix the situation that contributes to our fatigue. When we quit, we are actually being too short sighted. We are only thinking about resting in the moment without considering what the act of quitting holds in our future. For the Hebrews, the next forty years in the desert weren't any easier than the first 11 days. They gave up because they developed a negative attitude and lost sight of their dream; this did not make the rest of their life any easier.

Many people are like these Hebrews described in the Bible; they give up when their dreams and goals are right over the next ridge. They pursue their goals and actually get very close, only to quit in the final stretch of the road. Runners call this experience "The wall." They describe the feeling they get in a marathon when their bodies simply start to shut down around the twenty-three mile mark. These runners' bodies are telling them to quit the race. But runners know that if they push through the wall, they will get a "second wind" and be able to finish the race and achieve their goal.

Could you imagine if a person entered many marathons, only to quit each one after twenty-three miles? They could enter several marathons per year, train all the time, expend tons of energy and sacrifice, yet never achieve their goal of finishing. Doesn't that sound miserable? Yet this is exactly what many people do in life. They set goals, pursue them, only to quit because they get tired and weary about their ability to succeed.

In order to achieve your dreams, you must persevere even though your body, mind, or feelings are telling you otherwise. Doubt is a huge killer of the dreams that we have in our lives. You will always tend to face some type of "wall" in the progression of your dreams and goals. There is always a time in the pursuit of something great where we feel like we are going backwards. This is discouraging and contributes to our sense of being too tired to complete our journey. I promise you, keep moving forward and you will also get your second wind and realize your dreams.

Set definable goals

Dreams are essential because they give us the gut wrenching, emotional response that brings about the motivation to do something big. It was the dreams connected to sailing that led Regan and Cheryl to get to the point of breaking out of their routine and buying a boat. When they bought their sailboat they had dreams to sail to Hawaii. But dreams by their nature tend to be undefined. If they weren't careful they could pass that dream from year to year, while their boat never ventured far from the security of the marina.

Whereas dreams provide the necessary emotional component to start the process of achievement, goals provide the accountability. Goals are specific, definable, and measurable. Without goals attached to dreams, dreams will stay only as dreams, likely to never be realized. Honestly, this is what gives dreams a bad name. People see dreamers as simply "wishing" for something better, instead of making it happen.

A dream is saying, "Someday I want to sail to far away places." A goal is specific, such as "I am going to sail to Hawaii in July next year." A dream is a general direction–goals have specific coordinates and timelines. As soon as you attach specific details and a date to a dream, it becomes a goal.

Dreams are large and often lack general direction– goals have specific coordinates and timelines.

The pursuit and achievement of goals are essential for having a valuable life. Goals cause us to move towards something greater in life. When we pursue something better we have to discipline ourselves to make progress. As soon as you begin to purposefully discipline yourself in the pursuit of those goals, you become successful.

Sometimes the goals that are attached to our dreams are still so large and far away that we lack the belief that we can achieve them. Humans tend to need something tangible that they can believe in. One of the ways to accomplish this is to break the large goal down into bite-size pieces. Smaller goals along your journey can serve as a series of checkpoints to your dreams.

Doubt is a huge killer of the dreams that we have in our lives.

For example, Lets say that my dream is to lose weight and have a six-pack of abs instead of a keg. My large goal would be to lose 30 pounds and see the definition in my abs within 6 months. This is a great goal, but six months is a long time to wait and 30 pounds seems somewhat overwhelming. But, if I break down that goal into smaller achievements, I will be more likely to maintain my motivation. If I set a goal of losing 10 pounds in the next two months, that seems achievable to me.

So, we develop our dreams to get our minds to stretch far beyond where we would normally think. This causes us to develop strong emotion that will serve to motivate us towards movement. Then, we add the definition and timeline to those dreams to bring accountability to the process. Then, we break down those goals into checkpoints to help us stay motivated and keep on track. Finally, we take these smaller goals down to a daily goal. Regarding my goal for losing weight, my goal for today could be to not eat any sugary sweets. By setting smaller and smaller goals for ourselves along our journey, we increase our likelihood of ending up where we want to be.

Can we agree that you have a destiny? I'm not talking about fate or a predetermined destiny, just the fact that you will end up at a place based on the path you choose. Wouldn't you agree that it would be very good if the place where you arrived, happened to be the same place you want to be? This is not a given assumption for us. Just

In order to have our destiny and our goals align, we must be purposeful with our actions.

because we want to arrive in Hawaii, doesn't automatically mean that we will arrive there. It is even unlikely if we are drifting in our journey. In order to have our destiny and our goals align, we must be purposeful in the pursuit of our destiny.

So how do we chart the course for our goals so that we do not drift through life? First things first: You must set your goals and then make the decision to follow a path to your destiny that matches those goals. Your destiny will be the end result of a series of decisions you make.

Ralph Waldo Emerson is often given credit for the quote "Sow a thought and you reap an action; sow an act and you reap a habit; sow a habit and you reap a character; sow a character and you reap a destiny." There is some discussion that these words go even further back into ancient Buddhist teachings. Lets focus and expand on these foundational words of truth, but start from the results of your destiny and work backwards to what you need to be doing today to achieve that goal.

Your destiny will be based on the type of character you have developed throughout your life. Your destiny will follow your character because your character is consistent. Your character is like your autopilot, it drives you down a path without you having to think through every decision. In sports this is called muscle memory. An athlete practices often so that his or her body reacts automatically to the demand needed. You every wonder how a MLB player hits a ninety-five mph fastball? I will tell you this, he doesn't have time to think about what he is doing. Character is the same process for our minds. You will hit your successes out of the park when you train your character so that you do the right things without thinking about it.

Your character will be formed largely on the habits you have created. Habits are like consistent practice in sports. Practice doesn't make perfect, practice makes permanent. If character is automatic, habits are semi-automatic. Habits are still something we control, but because we do them consistently, they are second nature and easier to continue. Ever notice that the longer you engaged in a healthy behavior the easier it got? Pretty soon it just becomes a matter of your routine. Habits are powerful factors in forming who we will become. A good habit, however, can be broken within three days of inactivity. So the rule is, get a habit going and then keep it going until it becomes part of who you are.

So the rule is, get a habit going and then keep it going until it becomes part of who you are.

Your habits will be developed, based on the behaviors in which you engage on a consistent basis. If habits are semi-automatic, your behaviors are manual, such that each behavior is based on your decisions. Before a habit can be formed, it is necessary to discipline oneself to do the right things when the right things are uncomfortable or difficult. Ever go to the gym and begin to work out after months of not doing so? Remember how difficult it was to get your body moving and how sore you were afterwards?

Many people stay in the behavior management phase of success. They do the right behaviors, but not with enough consistency to form habits, which never solidifies into character. When people do not discipline their behaviors to the extent to form habits, they expend a great deal of energy for very little gain. The "Start, stop, start, stop" method of achieving goals develops more frustration than success. Imagine a man who goes to the gym with such irregularity that he only experiences the pain after a workout but never receives the benefit. Who would continue towards goals with that kind of results?

So, the consistency of your actions is a critical step in your journey to your goals. What forms your actions? Your words.

Your actions will be largely based on the words that you speak. When I took my three boys to an amusement park, my middle son, Hunter, was excited about hitting all the roller coasters. The more Hunter talked about the impending thrills, his older brother, Dakota, started talking about how he didn't like roller coasters. Dakota didn't really have any reason to be afraid of roller coasters, but guess how he acted by the time we hit the park? His behavior completely matched the words he had spoken repeatedly in the car.

As the day progressed at the park, Dakota started venturing onto some of the "calmer" rides and actually had fun. An interesting thing happened, he started talking about liking the thrilling rides. The more he talked about how much fun he was having, the more rides he added to his "willing to do" list. By the end of the day Dakota was raising his hands on the roller coasters, repeatedly. His actions directly followed the words that he spoke.

The words you speak will come from the thoughts that you think. This possibly sounds like an obvious statement. Of course what we say comes from our thoughts, but we only speak a fraction of our internal dialogue. If we allow our thoughts to be inconsistent with our goals it will only be a matter of time before we verbalize those thoughts.

The thoughts you have will come from input with which you program your brain. If you want to have positive thoughts it is absolutely necessary to surround yourself with positive people, read positive books, and listen to positive messages. If your son wanted to associate with a group of kids who have been expelled from school, you would probably be concerned about how your son would change–rightly so. Many adults falsely believe that they are immune to negative influences– they think they can watch or read whatever they want and still maintain productive thoughts. The truth is, kids are not the only ones who are influenced based on their exposure. You are what you read, like it or not.

Finally, the beginning of this process is what leads us to our input. The input you bring into your brain will be based on what you choose today. Your daily choices are the cornerstone of your goals. Everything you choose to do sets into motion a series of life-based building blocks that act like dominoes falling in a particular path. Your daily choices will lead to a particular destiny; it is within your power to determine if those choices lead to your goals.

Your daily choices are the cornerstone of your goals.

If I followed you around for just one day, would I be able to accurately conclude what your goals are? Most people do not achieve the things that they want in life because they undervalue the importance of today. The most common date to start a diet is "tomorrow." People mistakenly believe that if they are going to achieve a big goal, they are going to have to do something big. The truth is that the achievement of a big goal is going to be found in the disciplines of your daily habits. It is very important that your daily choices align with your goals and dreams, otherwise you might end up at a destiny that is not where you want to be.

The whole process looks like this:

Input → *Thoughts* → *Words* → *Behavior* → *Habit* → *Character* → Destiny

Daily
Choices

Goals /
Dreams

To successfully achieve your goals, you must ensure that what you do today, your input, your thoughts, your words, your actions, your habits, and your character all line up with what you want for your destiny. If you allow yourself to get off course on any of these steps, you will likely miss the things in life that you seek. You cannot drift and hope to make it to Hawaii, nor can you drift and hope to become successful. Success in anything starts with a large vision and ends with daily management. All of the steps along the way are within your control.

Don't should all over yourself

One of the reasons that many people resist setting goals is because they miss them. When people miss goals, sometimes they evaluate their "miss" as a "failure." This negative evaluation is reflective of a person turning goals into expectations. There is a huge difference between goals and expectations. Where goals are necessary, expectations can be fatal.

Let's say that my definition of success was shooting free throws in basketball. I know that this sounds silly, but people evaluate their worth on weirder stuff. Anyway, since I'm not a naturally gifted basketball player, I will set a number of baskets to be 70 of out of 100 shots. If I allow a goal of shooting baskets to become an expectation, I will draw a line between 69 and 70 successful shots. We can always tell if we set expectations by the use of the word "should", such as "I should be able to make 70 out of 100." This arbitrary line will define each shot as either a success or failure. Thus, if I shoot 70 baskets I'm successful, but if I make 69, I'm a failure.

The reason these expectations are fatal is due to the meaning we assign to them. With expectations, we apply standards of what we "should" be able to accomplish. These "should" statements actually have negative conclusions that we don't speak, but that are always present. If I make the statement "I should be able to make 70 out of 100 shots", the next hidden part of that statement says "Because any real man who has played basketball in his life would be able to hit 70 out of 100 shots. If I don't make at least 70 shots, I would be a lousy excuse for a real man."

So, I undergo my first trial of shooting free throws, but only make 21 out of 100. My conclusion, "That was horrible! I failed. I am bad at this." So I try again and get 19 out of 100. "Wow, I'm getting worse. What a failure." After the 10th trial, I have 30 out of 100. After the 20th attempt, I am only at 35 baskets out of 100 free throws.

Based on my aforementioned expectations with my "should" conclusions, my perspective of those twenty trials is, "Fail, fail, fail, fail, fail, fail ... twenty times." A person can only tell himself that he is a failure so many times before he decides to preserve what little self-image he might have left and quit. Such a person will often make excuses or rationalize about why basketball is not for him, how stupid it is, or that he was lied to about it being a good game.

So, identifying your use of the word "should" will help you realize when you are holding yourself or others to some type of arbitrary expectation. You might say, "I should have done better" or "Mike should have responded differently to that situation." Please be careful to not should all over yourself and others. When we do this, it causes one to shut down and stop trying. I, like you, don't want to see myself as a failure.

Why would I continue to stretch myself out of my comfort zone if I am going to feel criticized by either myself or someone else? And keep in mind, if I don't stretch out of my comfort zone, I won't grow.

It might be helpful for you to come to the realization that you are not perfect and you will never be perfect in anything. If you believe perfection is possible, you will live a life of guilt, self-criticism, and avoidance of new and different activities. The need for perfection is like trying to harness chaos into some logical order, it will be very frustrating and anxiety producing. You will probably never get everything right, so quit focusing on an artificial standard, to which you can never measure up.

Goals define a place of achievement to which we are hopefully growing.

Some people react negatively to the idea of dropping expectations. They think that if they don't have expectations, they will lose their edge or stop holding themselves to greater principles. This is not true because of the sense of failure, guilt, and shame that follow missed expectations. People can still hold onto ideals in life, but they need to approach them from a goal frame of reference, not one of expectation.

A goal orientation does not have the same conclusion of failure associated with expectations. Whereas having expectations causes us to evaluate each event as either a failure or success, goals define a place of achievement to which we are hopefully growing.

Lets use the same scenario of basketball outlined above, but this time we will set 70 baskets out of 100 shots as a goal. We will follow the same 20 trials of 100 shots each to understand the difference. In the first trial where I made 21 baskets out of 100, this is not considered a failure, only a starting point. The next trial of 19 baskets might be disappointing, but it is still not considered a failure, just another attempt. Even after the twentieth trial, I am only one half the way to what I set as a goal, but it is still not a failure.

You see, in a goal orientation, it is not about the individual trials, it is the overall direction we are going. So, even though I am only at 35 baskets after 20 trials, I am improving overall. I am shooting more baskets out of 100 than I was when I started practicing. This is success. I am getting better and I can continue to experience motivation towards the goal I set.

I honestly could continue to practice forever and never reach 70, maybe the closest I get is 65. But I got better and that is what setting goals in our lives is all about. It is about growing from where you are now into something more. If I never set a goal for 70 baskets, I would have never been able to improve off of my starting point.

If I approached basketball with an expectation perspective I would have quit at 35. But If I approached it from a goal orientation, I continue to feel good about my progress, I continue to get better, and accomplish much greater success.

So, being successful is all about the journey. As soon as you make the decision to change your current situation and pursue a worthwhile goal, you are successful. By simply reading this book and deciding to apply it in your life you are successful. You don't have to live a

Being successful is all about the journey.

perfect life, have the perfect marriage, or achieve a certain amount of wealth to consider yourself successful. Those are great areas for goals to pursue, but the action of moving towards them is where you are going to find value.

When I sit across from a hurting person or couple, the last thing they typically feel is successful. Mostly, this is because they don't understand success. Many times after I explain to them that they are successful because they have taken purposeful action to change their circumstances, I get back a blank look. This is such a key concept, however. If you do not allow yourself to feel successful until you achieve some type of result, life will be a constant negative experience. You will feel negative about yourself during the process because you haven't hit the "achievement" yet. Even if you stick with the program long enough that you achieve your destination, you will still be negative because the value is not in the attainment. You must allow yourself to feel like you are successful when you are in the hunt for your goals. This will keep you focused and energized to continue the pursuit. Once you identify where you are at and begin to make positive steps towards something better, you are successful.

Take Away Discussion Questions

1. What are the goals that are attached to your dreams?

2. When we set worthwhile dreams and goals and then lack the purposefulness to achieve them, this can be an extremely frustrating process. If you have experienced this, what happened?

3. Your dreams give you a glimpse into what your purpose is. What might this be for you?

4. If you leave your dreams in the "someday, somehow" category, they will probably never be realized. So take the possibility of failure and be willing to give dates to the things you want to accomplish in life.

5. Achieving your goals is going to be a purposeful event. You will have place value on the things that you think and do today. What is one thing you can discipline yourself to do every day that will lead to your goals?

6. If you see yourself as falling short of where you "expect" yourself to be, you will falsely conclude that you are a failure. What is an example of where you "shoulded over yourself."

7. Adversity does not destroy purpose–it strengthens it. How does this concept apply in your life?

8. You will not be able to achieve worthwhile goals from a position of comfort. What are some ways you can push yourself out of your comfort zone.

9. As soon as you set your sights on worthwhile goals in your life, you will be faced with some type of resistance. When has this happened to you?

10. Many times people quit right before their goals are realized because they get tired and weary. You have more reserve energy than you think you do. When have you proved this to be true in your life?

11. What is the one thing you are going to take away from this chapter and put into practice in your life, starting now?

Chapter 6

When You're Ripe, You're Rotten
The Principle of the Journey

> *We are at our very best, and we are happiest, when we are fully engaged in work we enjoy on the journey toward the goal we've established for ourselves. It gives meaning to our time off and comfort to our sleep. It makes everything else in life so wonderful, so worthwhile.*
>
> — *Earl Nightingale*

The year is 1920 and the economic situation of the United States seems strong. People are living large and playing hard. In many regards, the world seemed like an oyster ready to be harvested. A man emerged who capitalized on the common belief of the unending potential of America. His name, Charles Ponzi.

Carlo "Charles" Ponzi was born in, Italy 1882 and then immigrated to the United States at the young age of nineteen. Ponzi wandered from city to city working menial jobs for over fourteen years. It was in Boston during the year 1919 when Ponzi implemented his master plan to create wealth.

Ponzi had an idea for making money off of the exchange rates of postage. His plan involved foreign agents purchasing international postal coupons in countries with weak economies, then Ponzi exchanging them back into American funds. Ponzi claimed and promoted to the public that he netted profit on these transactions to the excess of 400 percent.

Ponzi's bragging caught the attention of eager investors. In 1919, Ponzi opened a business called The Security Exchange Company. Ponzi's concept seemed to be based on getting people to give him money with a promise that they would double their money in only ninety days.

Ponzi promoted a tempting business concept that promised huge rewards in a short timeframe, with no effort. Thousands of people lined up outside of his office to purchase promissory notes. The average investment is suspected to have been about three hundred dollars, worth approximately three thousand dollars in today's money. Ponzi's idea worked and it fueled eagerness with even more investors.

People believed Ponzi was legitimate because he made good on his promises to his early investors. Ponzi paid out the one hundred percent return on early investments by using the money from later contributors. Within only six months, Ponzi had taken in millions in investments, paid out his prior investors, and pocketed great sums of money. It is estimated that Ponzi had taken in one million dollars per week at the height of his scheme.

Ponzi's business started to generate some concern from local and federal authorities. But since Ponzi had managed to collect increasing sums of money to pay off prior investors, all his investors were happy. This soon changed. After only seven months in business, a news story broke on the front page questioning the legitimacy of Ponzi's business. He was shut down for one day until an auditor examined his books. Within hours, a mob of Ponzi's investors lined up outside his door demanding that they get their money back.

Ponzi settled nearly 1,000 claims to the panicked crowd and strongly opined that he had a legitimate and solid business and assured people their money was safe. When the anxious investors received their money back, Ponzi's public reputation was reaffirmed. People became enamored with Ponzi's successes, and he became a local icon.

This newfound support, however, crashed within one month. On August 10, 1920, the auditors, banks, and newspapers all declared Ponzi to be bankrupt. Three days later federal authorities arrested Ponzi.

An estimated forty thousand people had entrusted an estimated fifteen million dollars (about one hundred fifty million in U.S. funds today). Ponzi never used any of the money he received in his postage investment strategy, upon which his business was founded. Most people who invested their money with Ponzi, lost significantly.

The value of the prize is found in the price

Today, the Federal Trade Commission regulates such "business" models that follow Ponzi's "something for nothing" approach. Probably every year there is a new concept that promises people that they can get rich quick without putting forth any effort. These ideas are affectionately described as "Ponzi schemes." These models, like Ponzi's original proposition, always sound appealing to people who are looking for a big score without having to follow any principles of success. Also, similar to Ponzi's model, these schemes always collapse once they lose their initial excitement and investment. If something sounds too good to be true, it probably is.

If something sounds too good to be true, it probably is.

I remember talking to a man who just became involved in some type of "miracle cure" multilevel business. There will likely always be a business that promotes some type of fix-all developed from a twig found in the Amazon Rain Forest that will restore hair loss and cure diabetes. Every single time this happens, there are always groups of people who rally around the concept like it is what the world has always been waiting for. These businesses start up and tend to grow with exponential proportions. People join them; invest their money, and eagerly share with others their great returns.

These businesses can grow fast, but most always burst like a bubble. Typically, there are a couple factors that contribute to the collapse. Obviously, one of the downfalls occurs after the scientific community starts performing studies on the products. Once it is discovered that the claims were significantly over-hyped, the businesses tend to fade away. There are good and healthy products that truly will benefit us, but one should always be skeptical of a panacea. Such "fix alls" simply don't exist.

Another reason these businesses fail to sustain growth is that they are built on the foundation of "easy." As this particular man attempted to promote his new business, I learned that there was another business with a similar product that had started a few years prior. This man communicated with excitement about how people were abandoning the first business to jump into this new business because it gave them the opportunity to get in on the ground floor. He stressed the possibility of their success and shared with enthusiasm the story of a local doctor, who hadn't done anything, yet was making twenty thousand dollars per month because he got in early. This man didn't understand the concept that things that flash burn, burn out.

I politely smiled and nodded regarding his excitement because he wasn't asking for my opinion. But I clearly had an opinion. My opinion is that if a business grows by people jumping on board out of motivation based on looking for the latest and greatest thing, the business will die when those same people jump off when they think they see the next best thing coming around the corner. If a business is designed around people who are looking to not pay a price, it will always collapse. Fast success that does not last is no success at all.

I am not being critical of all businesses that have a multilevel design. There is legitimate business models that follow solid principles of success that have a recruiting component often misinterpreted as a pyramid scheme. The keys to identify a solid concept come down to the amount of real effort applied, such as sales of products or services, and steady sustainable growth. Increase can be based on

Fast success that does not last is no success at all.

excitement, but it will not remain if that emotion is based on hype. In short, there must be value as a foundation for the investment.

A solid business, like a solid person will grow with the corresponding price. It is much the same way that a house is built. There will be a large amount of time, work, and cost associated with the creation of plans, surveying and excavating the land, and the pouring of foundations. When all of that is done, the project doesn't yet look like a house. But what would happen if a builder was in such a hurry to start framing that he didn't bother with pouring a foundation? The house might get built, but it wouldn't last.

There is nothing glamorous about the foundation, the framing, wiring, or the plumbing in the construction of a home. When homebuyers walk through a house, their eyes catch the beautiful tile and the faux painting on the walls. The husband won't likely say to his wife, "Oh darling just look at the strength of that foundation." But that same couple will appreciate the strength of that foundation when their home stays square and true over the years. They will value the price that was paid by the builder to build the home without cutting corners out of the process.

There is something about human nature that continually gravitates us towards getting the results we want by some type of a shortcut. People get too end-oriented and develop destination disease. They want the rewards of success, but they believe that they can find a path where they will not have to pay a price.

A positive relationship exists between the amount of the price one has to pay and the significance of the prize that one receives. When people spend so much time trying to figure out how not to pay the price, they actually harm themselves by diminishing their rewards. You cannot take a shortcut to success without missing something critical along the way.

In order for something in our lives to have lasting value, it will take time and effort to create. Something that develops easily will fall apart easily. The Ash tree takes many years to grow to maturity. We use the wood of an ash tree to craft baseball bats that will withstand the impact of a 95 mph fastball. The Poplar tree will grow to 40 feet in just a few years, but its wood is so soft that the only thing it is good for is to chip up into paper pulp.

When people are focused on fast growth, unknowingly they are modeling their lives after the Poplar tree. They are too concerned about getting results fast, not understanding that this process weakens them. What good is it to be huge, if the first major wind storm that passes through will blow you over?

It is hard for us to delay our gratification. When we have dreams and goals of something big, we often want to see them unfold before our eyes, right out of the chute. When a woman decides she wants to lose 30 pounds, she wants to be 10 pounds lighter by next week. She might look for supplements that claim super results or fall prey to late-night infomercials that are pitching a new weight loss system. She might spend hundreds of dollars looking for a way to get the results she wants. This is why the weight loss business is a multi-billion dollar industry.

Have you ever noticed that people tend to yo-yo with weight loss? If somebody gets fast results through some type of miracle drug or diet, they will not likely maintain their results. This is because they didn't pay the correct price for losing the weight. They might have paid a financial cost, but they didn't pay the cost of self-discipline. Losing weight is honestly a fairly straightforward concept–expend more calories than you consume and your body will burn off what it has in storage. Thus, "the secret" to losing weight is found through a balanced diet, portion control, and physical exercise. If a person doesn't pay the price of learning these disciplines, any short-term results will never last.

To be successful in any aspect of life, individuals need to stop trying to negotiate their way around the price. Instead, such people should learn to embrace the price as part of their prize. If they think they can buy a Rolex on the streets of New York for one hundred dollars, they need to realize that it will be a fake. If they want a Rolex, they will have to pay the price for a Rolex. If they want a solid business, they must pay the price for a solid business. If it is personal growth they want, they cannot find it in a pill bottle–there is a price they will have to pay. Once we embrace the price, we can stop going around in circles looking for a shorter, easier path. Only after we understand the connection between the cost and the rewards will we appreciate the true value in the prizes we seek.

We need to learn to embrace the price as part of our prize.

Success is found in the journey

When does a person become successful? Is it when they earn their first million dollars? Hitting twenty years of marriage? Achieving salesman of the year? Reaching their ideal weight? Or is it after they finally get that degree? The answer is "no" to each of these results, because success is not a destination, it is a process. Success does not have anything to do with where you end up–it has everything to do with who you are becoming through the journey.

I have spoken with so many people who have destination disease. "I will be happy when …" Just fill in the blanks. The problem with this mentality is that all the focus gets centered on the results, usually at a sacrifice of the journey. They are looking for the great husband without the personal work required to attract a spouse of good quality.

Success does not have anything to do with where you end up–it has everything to do with who you become through the journey.

They are looking for the payload of wealth without the self-discipline to be responsible with it and the development of character to not let it destroy them. They are looking for the diet that will allow them to lose weight without changing their lifestyle. When people get focused on the results, they don't tend to grow. Thus, even when they get what they thought would make them happy, the results seem empty and unfulfilling. Then, they simply set their sights on the next thing that they believe will make them happy. If you do this, you are looking for happiness in all the wrong places. You will never find it if you are too focused on the finish line.

Success is similar to a marathon–the value is found in the accomplishment. Let's say that you want to finish a coveted race and get the reward, but you don't really want to train. So, there is an opportunity to step into the race in the final block. Simply jog for a few minutes and then cross the finish line. The trophy is presented to you and you take it home to display it on your mantle. How much value would that trophy hold? You might be able to show it off to impress some of your friends. It could even serve as some type of status symbol. But the fact that you know that you got the trophy without the struggle would diminish its value. Outside of its shiny metal shape, it would not represent anything meaningful.

You see, when most people finish a marathon, they are less focused on the trophy and more focused on the fact that they finished the race. It is the difficulty of the marathon that provides the value. If everybody could enter the race in the last block, the race would not mean anything. It is the fact that in order to finish such a race it takes physical and mental conditioning and a great deal of self-discipline. Because the goal is hard, only a small percentage of people actually do what it takes to accomplish it. Such people would rather have a tee shirt to remind them that they "did it" than a huge and valuable trophy that they could easily obtain.

Some people might think that I'm saying the finish line isn't important. Keep in mind that if there weren't a finish line in a marathon there would be very little point to the race. If there is nothing to win, there is no reason to go through the growth process. How many people would train and sacrifice to run twenty-six miles, just for the heck of it? Who would continue to push themselves to get better if it didn't matter how long it took to cross the finish line? Goals are essential and it is good for us to use those goals to direct our efforts. But, the value you will feel when you achieve a goal will not be found in the goal itself. The true value will be found in the personal satisfaction you have knowing that you overcame something in your life to get there.

Taking a gondola to the top of Mount Everest would be fun, but there would be no personal achievement in it. It is not getting to the top that equates to success, it is the discipline and overcoming that is required to make the journey that we value.

The growth through the process creates confidence. It is not unusual for people who have achieved great things to show good self-esteem. Often, when people see awards ceremonies associated with accomplishments, they . misinterpret confidence for arrogance. Clearly, sometimes individuals who achieve begin to read their own press clippings and get an inflated ego, but it's not always arrogance. Confidence in individuals will be present when they place their value on what they became through the process of reaching for their dreams. If each time individuals are knocked down they made a character-based decision to not give up, this creates strength. Emotions will attempt to convince them to stay down and quit. But when they persevered through the pain and struggle, their journey takes on more value than the trophy. That is why they value the trophy–it is all about what the trophy represents.

Joy is greater than happiness

There is a woman who came to see me once several years ago. The misery she experienced with her marriage contributed to her starting communication with an old boyfriend from high school. She identified herself as a religious person and said that she felt God was informing her that he wanted her to be happy. Leaving her husband and rekindling her high school flame could achieve happiness for her. She believed that she had "God's consent" in this decision based on the feeling of peace she experienced.

These kinds of situations tend to create a bind for me. Like many individuals, this woman talked about her decision as if she already knew the right answer. Her sharing this information seemed to be for the purpose of seeking confirmation, not seeking what was right. Getting someone to see a principle when they are not looking for one is tricky, if not impossible. I have found that the best I can do is ask a few pointed questions in the hopes that they will bite.

Regarding this woman's situation, it was interesting to me that she would believe God wanted her to leave her family to pursue a love interest, especially since her husband didn't reportedly do anything seriously wrong, such as cheating on her or abusing her or the children. Why would scripture constantly address the unity of marriage, only for God to go against this principle just to allow her to chase her own personal idea of happiness?

To me, using the name of God to justify and fulfill our own emotional desires or to avoid our fears, is the purest definition of blasphemy. Even Jesus was described as going against his emotion to follow principles. The Bible describes how Jesus felt fear when his crucifixion was pending, and he prayed to God to see if there was another way. Jesus showed a conviction to carry out God's will in spite of his own emotion. His emotion probably would have led him to catch the first donkey heading out of town. It is much easier to understand what God wants us to do by following established principles we know to be true.

After a few questions to this woman, she responded "But shouldn't I pursue things that make me happy? Doesn't God want me to be happy?" The simple answer to these questions is "no." This was not what she wanted to hear and disengaged from the conversation. Hopefully you are still with me. Now that I got your attention, I would like you to understand the difference between happiness and true joy or fulfillment in your life. When we pursue happiness, we tend to be shortsighted in things that we want right now.

"Buying that new Corvette will make me happy."

But not being able to pay all your debts after you buy that new Corvette will bring a lack of peace and security into your life. That short-term happiness will not translate into long-term joy. In the long run, living a balanced financial life will bring more joy than living under the pressure of bad financial decisions, even if you do have a lot of stuff.

If it were really that simple to achieve happiness, we would have a pill for it. In fact, that is why many people get addicted to a variety of drugs, such as Methamphetamine. They take the drug, and it temporarily fills the hole of unhappiness and insecurity. For a brief moment, they feel good about themselves–they feel happy. But, that feeling doesn't last. The aftermath of taking such a drug leaves them worse off than when they started. So, they fill the hole again with more drugs. Eventually, the drugs don't work anymore and they are simply maintaining their existence.

You probably don't take drugs, but when you make emotional decisions to get happiness, you are still getting a fix–a short-term fix. It's honestly the same thing. Some of your "fixes" are just as powerful as those drugs we were talking about. Did you know that relationships could be fixes? How about promotions? Sex? Avoidance? Whatever you do that gives you momentary relief from your pain or a sense of short-term pleasure will act as a fix in your life. The problem is, the more you place a Band-Aid over the issues, the bigger the underlying problems become.

One of the reasons we have such a high divorce rate in this country is because people believe they need to find happiness elsewhere. They change relationships in the pursuit of happiness instead of making the difficult changes that will ultimately bring a greater satisfaction and fulfillment into their lives. So they aptly swap out partners, but keep the underlying problems that led to their challenges to begin with.

Look for the course in your life that will bring a greater satisfaction and joy to you in the long run.

Instead of pursuing things that you believe will make you happy, look for the course in your life that will bring a greater satisfaction and joy to you in the long run. Disciplining yourself now to not give in to your emotional needs will bring you much greater rewards in the future.

Take Away Discussion Questions

1. Regardless of the rewards you seek in life, you must understand that you can achieve them, if you are willing to pay the price. What examples can you think of where you or others attempted to use a shortcut?

2. Paying towards your future is not as costly as if you wait for the consequences of the easy path. A payment up front will usually be in the form of some type of sacrifice that you have to make. What could this look like for you?

3. Consequences for bad decisions have a potential to cost us much more than we could ever anticipate. They can be devastating and even extend into our children's lives. What examples have you seen of this?

4. Do you feel like you are paying a productive price in your life now? Or are you paying for the consequences of past non-productive decisions?

5. Life is predictable; it always is made up of compensations. What you give out is exactly what you will receive. What are you willing to pay to realize your potential?

6. Your price might be different than someone else's. You could have to pay more because of prior choices you made, or things you haven't learned yet. What might contribute to this for you?

7. Results are exponential. If you only increased your price by ten percent, you would notice a significant difference in your life. If you increased your effort by a consistent twenty percent, the results you would get in your life would be astounding. What would a ten or twenty percent increase look like for you?

8. The hardships you have gone through have served a purpose in your life, even though you don't always see it at the time. What hardships have you gone through to prepare you for greater victories in your life?

9. Like the athlete who looks forward to feeling the burn of her muscles and the sweat running into her eyes, you too can change your perception to the price you pay for victory in your life. What is a way you can redefine some of the pains you've experienced?

10. The problem when individuals choose happiness over growth is that they will miss out on the greater feelings of joy down the road. What are some examples of this?

11. What is the one thing you are going to take away from this chapter and put into practice in your life, starting now?

Chapter 7

You Are a Boomerang
The Principle of Compensation

*The fight is won or lost far away from witnesses –
behind the lines, in the gym, and out there on the road,
long before I dance under those lights.*

— *Muhammad Ali*

When my oldest son Dakota entered junior high school
he started his journey at the registration circus with his mom.
As they strolled past the table display for various sports,
Dakota turned to Laura and said, "I want to play football."
Laura reported feeling somewhat shocked because Dakota
doesn't exactly like to run, but she said "okay" and they
signed him up. When they got home, I had a similar reaction
to Laura's. I talked with Dakota about what being on the
football team would probably be like. I informed him of the
hard work and getting hit and knocked down by other
players. Dakota listened and was respectful, but his focus on
being part of the team overrode his attention to our words. I
explained to Dakota that he would have our support if he
wanted to join the team, but my condition was that he had to
commit to the entire season. Dakota naively agreed, and he
became a football player.

It wasn't but one week into the season when Dakota
regretted his decision. He had never played football before

and struggled with understanding the game. Added to this was the fact that he is not a gifted athlete. He didn't like the running drills, and he didn't like getting knocked down throughout the practices. Dakota consistently came in last during the running relays and didn't get much time playing in the games. Knowing how cruel young adolescents can be, there were many of the other players who picked on Dakota and told him that he should just quit.

It was right after his first game that Dakota cried the entire ride home, saying that he hated football and wanted to quit. My comment to him in the car was "That's too bad Dakota, but you committed to finishing out the season, so you can't quit." This comment escalated Dakota's hysterics. He reported to feel the worst he ever had in his life.

I later came to Dakota and talked with him about how we sometimes have to make tough decisions, even if we don't feel like it. I gave him an out, a chance to quit the team. But I shared with him that if he quit, I couldn't respect his decision and he would likely lose the respect of his coaches and teammates. Dakota thought it over and talked to his coach the next day. Out of that meeting, he shared with me that he committed to his coach that he would give it another two weeks, and then decide if he was going to stay or quit.

I sat Dakota down and told him that I was proud of him for making a tough decision. Then I told him that I would make a deal with him. I promised him that if he gave one hundred percent in practice over the next two weeks–meaning that he ran his hardest, kept a positive attitude, encouraged the other kids, and picked himself up when he got knocked down–his coach would notice and he would turn his football experience into something positive. I found the movie *Rudy*, about the Notre Dame Football player, and we studied together what putting heart into football looked like. Dakota agreed that he would give one hundred percent for two weeks.

Dakota held to his part of the deal and really put forth a strong effort. He still ran as one of the slowest kids on the

team and never got much playing time, but he ran his
hardest, never complained, and picked himself right off the
ground when he got knocked on his butt. His mom and I
noticed a big difference in his effort and we both told him
that we were proud of him.

A week hadn't even gone by when Dakota came to me
and said, "Dad, you lied to me." I reacted with some shock as
I asked, "How?" He could no longer contain his smile and
said, "You told me that if I put my heart into the practices, in
two weeks the coach would notice. It only took three days!"
Dakota explained that on that day's practice, it was especially
difficult. The weather was miserable and the attitudes of the
players were negative. After the practice ended, the head
coach responded with clear frustration towards the team.
Dakota said his coach sat the team down in the end zone and
went off on them. During part of the coach's rant, he
reportedly said to them, "You guys aren't putting your heart
into this, you are fighting with each other and you are not
acting like a team. Every single one of you needs an attitude
like Dakota's. Do you see how he gets knocked down and gets
right back up with a positive attitude? If we all had Dakota's
heart, nobody could stop us!"

Dakota was part of the team at that point, and he never
talked about quitting again. The thing was, the positives
didn't stop coming. Each week during the rest of the season,
Dakota shared how somebody said something positive to him.
One week, one of the senior players on the team told him in
the locker room, "Dakota, you're tough. I was sure you were
going to quit." It ended up that Dakota won the respect of
probably ninety percent of the team.

When the season wrapped up, the team had really come
together. Dakota never did get much playtime during the
games, but he was part of the team, and that was what he
really wanted. I showed up for one of the last practices and
stood along the sidelines. The head coach saw me and made
his way over to talk to me. He said, "I just wanted to let you
know that I selected Dakota for the Sportsmanship Award.

This is a school-wide athletic award and I get to pick one
player to nominate. I chose Dakota because of how he
contributed to this team. His dedication and perseverance
helped bring the team together. I'm going to announce my
decision to the whole team after practice."

On the ride to school the next day, Dakota and I talked
about his football experience. I asked him, "Why do you think
your football season turned from being so negative to so
positive?" Without hesitation, Dakota answered, "God's laws."
I asked him to explain. He said, "Dad, you told me about
God's law of compensation and how it always holds true. That
is why you promised me good results if I put my heart into
football. I trusted you and put my heart into practice, and
God's law was there to give me
the results just like you said."

*"It is one of the most
beautiful compensations
in life that no man can
sincerely try to help
another without helping
himself."*

—Ralph Waldo Emerson

The truth is, I thought
that if Dakota put his heart
into practice like we talked
about, he might get a passing
comment or a pat on his
helmet from the coach. The
rewards that flowed into
Dakota's life with this
application were far greater
than I had even imagined. I believe that Dakota will
remember the power of how his perseverance and positive
attitude paid off for him throughout his entire life.

I refer to this law as the law of compensation. Simply put,
you get back what you put out.

The Law of compensation is universal

The law of compensation is a universal law that crosses all
religions and belief systems. Every belief system has a name
for the same principle. In Christianity it is called the Law of
Sowing and Reaping. In the book of Galatians it states, "Do
not be deceived, God is not mocked. For whatever a man

sows, that he will also reap." In Buddhism and Hinduism the same principle is called the law of Karma, or moral causation. From ancient Zen teachings to new age philosophies, the same principle is called the Law of Cause and Effect or the Law of Attraction. Probably the most common definition of this principle is the Golden Rule.

With acceptance of this principle across so many different belief systems, it probably qualifies as the most widely accepted principle on the planet. The principle simply states that there are universal properties that connect all people and all things. Whether you call this energy, aura, or the Holy Spirit, it pretty much comes down to the same thing–interconnectedness. Once we accept that everything in the universe is connected, we can understand that our actions do not occur in isolation. Through this process of interconnection, what happens to one thing must affect another. How we think and what we do to others is connected to what happens to us. As Ralph Waldo Emerson put it, "It is one of the most beautiful compensations in life that no man can sincerely try to help another without helping himself." The reverse of this is also true–when we hurt others we ultimately hurt ourselves.

It was at least fifteen years ago when my wife Laura and I were traveling through New England by car. We drove into the town of Salem, Massachusetts. Much to our surprise, we discovered that the legacy of Salem's history of witches continued to be strong in our current culture. Salem had the image of a cute and well-maintained town that looked like many other tourist destinations. The town displayed shops and small courtyard restaurants–and witches. It seemed like every street had a potion maker, spell crafter, fortuneteller, Tarot card reader, or spiritual advisor. It was a little disconcerting, and we couldn't help but wonder if all the different businesses were simply capitalizing on Salem's rich history.

In one of our stops we struck up a conversation with a well-dressed woman in her fifties, who identified herself as a witch and added that she owned one of the shops in town. No warts on the nose, no black hat or broom—she was pleasant, friendly, and happily engaged us in conversation. Being a naturally curious person and knowing nothing about witches, I started firing questions at her. "Are there good witches and bad witches?" I asked her. She confirmed that this is actually the case. She stated that there are witches who use their energy for good, and those who use it for bad. She said that spells do exist, but good witches would never consider casting something on somebody that would cause harm. She explained that all witches believe that whatever energy is cast out, it comes back in greater force onto that person. So, she reasoned that if she were to cause somebody harm though her negative energy, she would receive back more bad things on her. She said that witches who practice in the dark side of this energy fall into a trap of doing bad things, getting more bad things coming into their own lives, and trying to overcome those consequences by doing more bad things. She said, "It is a cycle that cannot be won."

I might disagree with this woman to the source of the law of compensation, but I have to admire her submission. She clearly understood and lived her life according to the principle. The law of compensation has been described in most every religion and philosophy. It has as many names as there are different names for God. This principle has been defined so many times by such diverse people because of the consistency of the results. It is important to understand that compensation, like all of God's laws are not whimsical or individualized—there is order, reason, and a universal application to them. A great architect of the universe has created them and they apply to everyone, even you.

We always harvest what we sow

Imagine along with me, what the results could have been with Dakota if he had made different decisions? What would his experience have been if he had gone through with his initial desire of quitting the team or if he didn't choose to have a good attitude? It could have carried a negative chain of events in his life for a long time.

That's exactly what happened to Fred. Fred is a thirty-seven-year-old divorced father of an eight- year-old girl. To summarize Fred, he is a guy with unbelievable potential, who has spent his whole life operating off his emotions. Thus, his potential is largely untapped. I had been having an ongoing discussion with Fred about the Law of Compensation and how he constantly gets negative results in his life because of his behavior. I shared with Fred the story of Dakota's football experience as an example of this law.

Fred read my story about Dakota, and when he put it down he said, "I have a baseball story just like this, but with a completely different outcome." Fred went on to share his story, "When I was in sixth grade, I tried out for baseball and did good enough to be placed on a more advanced team. But, I didn't have the skill level to perform on that team, and I was miserable. I didn't get one hit all season and I felt like a failure. So I quit. I know that I lost the respect of my dad, of the coach, and of my teammates. I had such a disdain for sports after that point that I never played a sport again. Right after I quit, I stopped hanging around with the athletes and good kids, and found an accepting association with the drinking and the drug-using crowd. Within eighteen months of quitting that baseball team, I took my first drink. I was accepted into that association and became one of the 'stoners' in school. Since that time, my life has been filled with alcoholism and drug addiction and running away from everything. I have never finished anything I started. I can't believe that I can trace this pattern in my life back to when I was eleven!"

Every individual must take a position of personal responsibility to plant their own field if they want a specific harvest.

Fred concluded, "I need to break this cycle in my life and start putting into life the things that I want to get back. I don't want to be a quitter anymore." Fred understood that if he wanted a different life for his future, he would have to sow different attitudes and behaviors into his life from this point on.

Imagine a farmer has a field, and he is going to plant some type of crop. In the beginning all he has is a field of dirt, but he wants a crop of corn. Which strategy to achieve his goal would be in his best interest–for him to plant the field himself or wait for corn to appear some other way? It is possible I suppose, that somebody could come by offer to plant his field with their corn seed. But such a passive strategy is a long shot to achieve any goal. It is his field, and if he wants a specific crop he has the ability to seed it himself.

The thing is, a harvest of corn is a metaphor for a harvest of success in any other area of life. Many people sit by their field and believe that the lack of their crop is based on circumstances beyond their control–what somebody else did or didn't do. Thus, they wait and wait for good things to happen, instead of making it happen themselves. Every individual must take a position of personal responsibility to plant their own field if they want a specific harvest.

Additionally, many people do sow their own seeds, but don't attend to what types of seeds they plant in their field. It's almost like they don't connect what they use for seed to what they end up harvesting. If you used the seed that you had stored in your barn because it was easy and readily available, what would you get? If your field produced wheat, there is no question about it, you used wheat seed. What would you get if you wanted a crop of corn, but still used the seed in your barn? You would still get a harvest of wheat. What about if you really, really, really wanted corn? Still wheat. The harvest you get in your field will be exactly what you sow into the ground.

Many great leaders seem to have a strong understanding of compensation. Abraham Lincoln focused on the law of compensation when it came to an address on slavery. He said, "This is a world of compensations; and he who would *be* no slave, must consent to *have* no slave. Those who deny freedom to others, deserve it not for themselves; and, under a just God, can not long retain it." Lincoln was saying that if we enslave others, God's law of compensation would enslave us, not necessarily with metal chains, but with other forms of bondage. Lincoln stressed the truth that one cannot escape the consequence of our actions.

You see, the law of compensation exists for so much more than just crops in a field. The law of compensation applies to all aspects of our lives. We are constantly sowing some type of seed. We sow positive seeds of compassion, love, grace, forgiveness, and respect. But we also sow negative seeds of selfishness, hate, judgment, resentment, and disrespect. These seeds produce harvests in our lives. If we don't like the harvest, we need to start the evaluation process by examining our seed.

You are responsible for your own harvest

I believe most people intuitively accept the principle of compensation to some degree. They want to believe that if they do good things, good things will happen to them. Yet, most people don't live their lives like this with any degree of consistency. I don't believe that they fully understand the fact that the law of compensation never fails. If they did, I believe they would be more careful about what they put out into life.

One way to put this in perspective is to imagine that I present a person with a magical machine. This machine simply duplicates whatever she puts into it. If she puts a banana in the slot, three bananas come out the other side. Think about the possibilities of such a machine. If this individual put one thousand dollars into the machine, pushed a button, and boom, she would have three thousand dollars. A person could sit there and put all the things she wanted into the machine, and the machine would multiply her desires. But the machine doesn't only work for the positive–it duplicates everything that is put into it. If this woman had some garbage she didn't want, she might try and get rid of it by sticking it into the machine. This would not be a good idea because the machine simply produces three times more of what she didn't want.

With this kind of immediate results, a person would absolutely use such a machine only to her advantage. She would not hesitate to take her last one hundred dollars and give it to the machine to get three hundred dollars back. She would also never even consider putting something in the machine that she didn't want. Would anybody put debt into the machine? How about dishonesty? Nobody would want more debt or people lying to him or her. Therefore, nobody would be foolish enough to put those things into the machine. It's a simple rule, whatever you put in you get back in greater amounts.

It's a simple rule, whatever you put in you get back in greater amounts.

So what is the difference between such a machine and the law of compensation? The law is similar, but not regarding the timing or the exactness of the results. See, the law of compensation doesn't necessarily have an immediate payback, like I presented with the machine. It could be days, months, or even years before a person is compensated for what she has sown in her life. Thus, people tend to disconnect the results they harvest in their lives with the sowing behavior that they engaged in previously.

So because of the lack of immediate feedback, people fail to guard what they sow, and they put things into the machine that they don't want. They don't want conflict, yet they go through life fighting. They want people to be honest with them, yet they lie to others. They demand respect, but they don't treat people with respect. An individual cannot put unwanted things into the machine and get what they want. This violates the law and it will never work.

In addition, the law of compensation does not necessarily return exactly the form of what an individual puts in. So, if a man sows money directly into charity, he probably will not have a harvest by someone giving him charity. A multiple of the money he sowed will not fall from the sky and land in his pocket. Instead, he might get a harvest of opportunity or ideas, which he could then use to produce an abundance of money. Remember, when we sow corn seed into the ground, we don't get a harvest of corn seed; we get a harvest of corn. We have to take that harvest, process it, use some of it, sell some of it, and set some aside to use in future planting.

So, if I lie to somebody, it doesn't necessarily mean that that person will eventually lie to me. If a person lies, he is sowing seeds of dishonesty, self-centeredness, and avoidance of responsibility. These seeds will come back to him in a variety of ways. He might attract dishonest people into his life, somebody else might use him for their own personal gain, or people he wishes to trust him might treat him with suspicion, without really understanding why. This man might reap a harvest of feeling like he never gets any breaks in life.

Sometimes we fail to recognize how we are contributing to our problems. Not too long ago I was speaking with a man in the middle of a nasty custody battle. He complained that somebody called into his work and accused him of being a child molester. This led to tensions with his employer and the request that he find employment elsewhere due to the high drama and conflict going on in his life. When he brought this horrible situation up, honestly I wasn't the least bit surprised that it happened. Why? Because a few months earlier he called Child Services and made an allegation that his children were being abused in their mother's care. When I pointed out how he reaped the conflict very similar to what he had sowed, he struggled to see the connection. He reasoned that he was legitimately concerned about the welfare of his children and he didn't get anybody fired. Remember what I

said about how we will always reap more than we sow?
Conflict begets conflict, no matter how you might try and
justify it.

If a person wants to sting somebody with spite or
vengeance, he should try and remember the law of
compensation as it applies to the honeybee. If a honeybee
stings somebody, that act of aggression terminates its life.
There was an immediate compensation onto the bee that was
much greater than what the bee inflicted on its target. It is
very similar to the old adage, "He, who
lives by the sword, dies by the sword."

*Conflict begets
conflict, no
matter how you
might try and
justify it.*

When bad stuff happens in our
lives, it is so much easier to find a
reason or explanation for it outside of
ourselves. It is much more
uncomfortable too look in the mirror.

If a man's wife is irritated with him, it is
a quick and easy rationale for him to state that she is
hormonal or emotionally irrational. It is much harder to
examine if he has loved her and is giving her what she needs.
Could her distance be related to his lack of communication?
He would have to ask himself, "When was the last time I told
her she was beautiful?" Is it possible that he has not been
feeding her emotionally and that starving pattern has led to
her negative reaction toward him? According to the law of
compensation, that is highly possible.

I've talked to parents who are struggling with a
disrespectful child. Most of the time such parents are looking
for increased discipline measures to get their kids in line. The
problem is, the more authoritarian these parents get, and the
less respectful they act towards their child. The more they act
with disrespect, the more they get disrespectful attitudes from
their child. I have to explain to these parents all the time that
they need to have consistent discipline for their child in such
a way that their child relates the consequences with what he
or she has done. If the parents wish to reap a harvest of
respect from their child, they need to understand that they

have to sow respect when they administer the discipline to their child.

Looking in the mirror is not an enjoyable perspective. Parents especially don't like to examine their own behavior when they are looking for their kids to come under more control. It is much easier to see the behaviors of others as not connected to our own.

"I just want her to change. She is the problem, not me. I would treat her with more love if she wasn't such a grump."

I'm sorry, but that is like saying that the farmer should wait to plant his corn seed until his field first produces a harvest of corn. I believe he would wait a long time for corn to come out of nothing. If the farmer doesn't get a harvest of corn, there is one place to look–the mirror.

It's time each and every person took responsibility for the good, the bad, and the ugly in our own lives. It's not our parents' fault. Many people have very legitimate examples of parents, who were a negative influence in their lives. One or both of them may have even been abusive or neglectful. Some people have gone through some horrible things in life, yet they still make their own choices now. Making good choices might be more difficult because of negative experiences growing up, but anybody can still make good choices. Good choices will produce good results.

Take Away Discussion Questions

1. The law of compensation is universally accepted. Why do you think people don't live consistently with this principle?

2. Do you sow negative thoughts about yourself? How will you ever feel better about yourself when you are constantly cutting yourself down? What are some examples of your negative seed?

3. Please realize that you can produce the results you want in any area of you life if you become purposeful in what you sow. In what way are you going to increase your purposeful direction?

4. The law of compensation is like a magical machine. What is something you feed into your machine that produces more of what you don't want?

5. Do you want better relationships? How does the law of compensation apply in this area?

6. Learn to love God, love yourself, and love others. How does growing in these areas lead to sowing the right seeds and getting the harvest of your heart.

7. Understand that it takes a step of faith to sow the right things in life. In order to do the right things, it sometimes feels like we are exposing ourselves to unnecessary vulnerability. Have you ever experienced this? How?

8. If you have conflict in your life, it is difficult to sow love when you believe that others will use you up and spit you out. Love anyway, because even if the person with whom you are in conflict does not receive your love, you will still reap love back into your life. How does this concept apply in your life?

9. Don't fall into the trap of believing that you have anything to do with the cultivating process of the harvest. Your responsibility is simply to sow the correct seed. God will grow it. What examples can you think of that illustrate this.

10. Step out in faith and understand that it is never wrong to do the right things. How can you find peace in this understanding?

11. What is the one thing you are going to take away from this chapter and put into practice in your life, starting now?

Chapter 8

Nobody Likes to Admit They Are Lost
The Principle of Truth

> *Truth is by nature self-evident. As soon as you remove the cobwebs of ignorance that surround it, it shines clear.*
>
> — *Mohandas Gandhi*

Ryan and Lori lived in the Midwest and were visiting a major metropolitan city for their vacation. When they arrived at the airport they rented a car and drove to their hotel. The darkness of the night combined with heavy rain on the windshield made driving difficult. The city seemed alive with commotion as the heavy traffic filled with commuters returning home from the tall downtown office buildings.

As Ryan made his way in the direction of the hotel, he mistakenly took the wrong exit. Lori suggested that they stop and get directions, but Ryan insisted that he knew where he was and could find his way. With every turn that he made, it seemed to get darker, dirtier, and further from where he wanted to be. They were soon seeing cars that had been stripped of their tires as well as graffiti tagging the steel barriers to the rundown stores. They each checked to make sure that the doors of their rental car were locked.

Ryan kept turning and turning, trying to find his way to their hotel. He turned off the radio so that he could concentrate his attention to his driving. Ryan's heart began to pound stronger in his chest as he felt the danger of his surroundings. He saw people standing on the side of the road, warming themselves over a burning barrel. Ryan noticed that as they drove slowly by, the people on the street were watching their every move. He felt the sense of danger and didn't even want to stop at a light for fear of his surroundings. Lori found a map in the glove compartment and attempted to evaluate where they were under the dim dome light. Their tone with each other got more pointed and less productive.

"Why don't you just turn around and get back to the freeway!" Lori stated with apparent frustration.

With his building irritation he barked at her, "That is what I'm trying to do!"

"You're lost!" she accused.

"I am not!" he defended "I know that this road will lead us downtown and to our hotel."

It was outwardly apparent that he stopped listening to Lori and that her comments weren't making their situation any better. The more she tried to reason with him that he didn't know where he was going, the more defensive Ryan became, telling her they were fine. She reported feeling hopeless when they drove past the same group of dangerous looking people and Ryan failed to recognize that he had just made a huge loop. It was now an hour later and they were still driving in circles, running out of gas, and risking their lives.

Why did this couple keep going around in circles? They had a goal of getting to their hotel and having a great vacation. Lori even had a map that could show them exactly what turns to make to achieve their goal. The problem was that Ryan refused to acknowledge that he was lost. He kept going around the same non-productive route. In order for this couple to find their hotel, they would have to admit that what they were doing was non-productive and identify exactly where they were. Once they have the starting point, they can plot the most direct route to their goal.

Convincing yourself that you are not lost will keep you lost

How long would an individual be willing to retrace the same meaningless steps without achieving their goals? Hopefully, not long. Unfortunately, this describes a large number of people. Many wandering soles spend a great deal of energy convincing themselves that they are in the right place or doing the right things. It is not that people don't want better things to occur in their lives. They do. They simply believe that they can achieve the success they want in life without having to change. Thus, they continue to engage in the same patterns over and over again, just expecting that the next time they turn that corner, the achievement of their goals will somehow be there.

Change frightens people. One of the greatest fears of man is the fear of the unknown. People are comfortable with what they know, even if it is negative. So, though the path they have established doesn't produce the treasure they seek, at least they are familiar with the path. The idea of admitting that they have been following the wrong path would require a great deal of humility. Many people are way too prideful to admit that they have been doing something that doesn't work. So they rationalize to themselves that they are the right person and they are doing the right things, the map is just not accurate.

Just because people are in negative situations does not mean that this is what they want. Many individuals are not living according to their desires, yet don't change because the path they are on is all they know. I have seen women stay in abusive relationships because they were uncertain about what their life would be like if things changed. They wonder if they could survive financially on their own or they believe that they would never find another man to love them. These women do not want to stay in abusive relationships. They are not masochists who enjoy being abused—they honestly feel trapped. So, they develop a sense of hopelessness and give in to the path they see for their life.

There are a great number of people who use rationalization or justification to explain why they can't or shouldn't change. If they were to admit that they were lost, they would have to face the fact that they were doing something wrong. It is easier to blame fate, God, luck, skill, talent, race, sex, or even our parents for being on the wrong path. When someone blames his or her position in life on something else, it gives a seemingly legitimate excuse why change is not possible. If they see their fate as determined based on being from the wrong side of the tracks, why try to change something that is already set? Many young gang members see their destiny as joining a gang, and they openly admit that they will not likely live into their twenties. Most of them never even try to avoid that perceived fate in their lives.

When people follow a familiar path, they often mistake familiarity for functionality. A person might say, "I'm not lost, I recognize that building." The reason he recognized that building was because he had been driving circles around it. Just because he is familiar with the route he is taking, does not mean that it will lead to his goals. In fact, most of the time the necessary journey requires us to venture into unknown territory to reach the destination we seek in life.

The necessary journey requires us to venture into unknown territory to reach the destination we seek in life.

Unknown paths are often uncomfortable. When we find ourselves on a journey that feels awkward, this experience of discomfort causes us to gravitate back to the familiar. So each time we start actually heading towards our goals, it is very easy to jump back into a dysfunctional pattern and once again justify how familiar equals functional.

I would say that even the majority of individuals who seek counseling or mentorship don't really want to fully admit the nature of their struggles in life. They clearly feel pain in their lives, and they want the hurt to stop, but many times they want simple solutions without having to face their fears or give up their desires. It is like they want to hear, "No, you are right, and you deserve to feel that way, we need to change the world."

This concept of justifying the familiar path was evident in a couple referred to me for marriage counseling by their pastor. Jay and Alice had been married for over thirty years and most of the people who knew of them saw them as the model couple. They were both active in their church. Jay served as an usher, Alice ran food drives, and they co-led a Sunday school class. Their marriage, however, was a mess.

Jay and Alice were both miserable. They shared a home, a couple of boys who were grown and gone, and a few grandchildren, but not much else. Jay was successful in his business dealings and directed his life with his dominate personality. Jay is a good example of someone who refused to acknowledge that the path he was living was not working. He came to counseling with his wife as an attempt to have someone else try and point things out to her. Jay believed that his perspective was correct and that if Alice only agreed to do what he said, everything would be fine. Jay saw his controlling and even aggressive behavior as "leadership."

It seemed that no matter what was communicated during their sessions, Jay only applied the information to his existing perspective that he was right. He literally twisted everything and interpreted things out of context. For example, when I told Jay that he needed to insulate his wife from some of the stress in their lives he took it upon himself to remove her from even more of his business decisions and suggested that she not come to the office anymore. Jay's behavior clearly left Alice feeling more disconnected and insecure in their relationship.

Over the months of sessions spent with Jay and Alice, Jay would not admit that he was failing in his role as a husband. He continued to focus on how Alice was needy and impossible to please. Jay honestly believed that his "great leadership skills" would be more evident if Alice only did what she was supposed to do. He said many times, "Todd, I know what is right, I know what to do. We just have to get Alice to get on board."

Unfortunately, because Jay thought he was somewhere else in his personal growth and skill set, he never was able to embrace the tools to help change his relationship. The bottom line became that Jay was unwilling to accept personal responsibility for his part in their loveless marriage. He stuck to his own perspective and never humbled himself to admit that he was lost. As a result, Jay and Alice are in the same place in their relationship as they were before they sought help–possibly even worse.

When we put in effort and time to try and achieve a goal, only to have results of failure, it can feel like the possibility of change is impossible. The more times we spend driving around in circles, the more hopeless we can become. Do it long enough and eventually the conclusion is drawn that things will never get better. Once we believe nothing will change, we are right.

Once we believe nothing will change, we are right.

Unfortunately, the conclusion of why change was not attained is usually based on faulty logic, such as "It just can't work," "The advice was bad," or "You can't teach an old dog new tricks." Finding external explanations for our results will only keep us lost.

Everybody has some degree of the denial pattern that Jay promoted. You might say, "But Todd, that guy had serious issues that anybody could see. I don't control my wife or act that way." That might be true, but everybody has non-productive patterns in their lives. We typically never have a challenge seeing where somebody else is struggling, yet we have major blind spots for weakness in our own lives.

Part of the problem is that we are too close to our own lives to see them objectively. The emotion we have about where and who we are clouds our ability to see things rationally. For example, the husband drove around in circles in the dangerous part of town and refused to admit that he was lost because if he admitted he didn't know where he was going, he would have to face the fact that he failed. If he saw his actions as failing, he might evaluate himself to be a failure as a husband, and even as a man. Nobody wants to face such vulnerable conclusions. So he tries to demonstrate his competence by being short with his wife and driving in circles while acting like he knows what he is doing. Clearly, this is not a logical process. Anybody standing on the outside would be shaking their heads, yet when we are in the middle of the patterns, we fail to see it. As a result, we go deeper and deeper into trouble.

You can be 90 percent right and 100 percent wrong

Nobody on the planet does something 100 percent right. Even the experts in any area do not perform perfectly. Everybody has blind spots that prevent him or her from seeing the truth in their lives. Because people are not machines, they cannot see things with complete objectivity. In fact, the more emotionally vested we are with something, the less clearly we can see the truth. I have provided counsel to hundreds of couples to help them understand each other, yet I miss things in dealing with Laura all the time.

It is normal to have areas of weakness and challenge. The key is to simply be honest with us about where those areas of challenge exist. When we fail to recognize weakness, we stay in a place of being weak.

Once a person finally gets to a point in their life were they are willing to admit that they are lost and thus not on track with their goals, it can seem like an overwhelming process to change everything. As they get their life on track, most of the time they correct the most significant areas of the problem. In general, however, people change just enough to make the pain go away. As soon as they feel the results of a course correction in their life, they tend to stop their productive energy. They might deal with 90 percent of that issue in their life, but the last 10 percent just isn't addressed.

The more emotionally vested we are with something, the less clearly we can see the truth.

Only dealing with 90 percent of the issue is like cutting yourself with a dirty knife and then only cleaning out 90 percent of the wound; or a surgeon only getting 90 percent of the cancerous cells. This is going to cause problems. Don't get me wrong, a person should be commended for their effort–90 percent is better than not dealing with it at all. But if an individual is going to address the issues, why not deal with all of it? Why fool oneself into believing that the problem has been addressed, only to have it resurface in some other way?

Remember when antibiotics were prescribed for 14 days? The physician tells the patient "Take one pill each day for the next two weeks." How long does the typical person take their daily pills? Until the pain goes away. If the physician wanted them to discontinue their prescription after the pain subsided, that would have been on the bottle.

Most people, who do face negative patterns in their life, still hold back in facing all of it. For example, a man might recognize that he has a drinking problem and vow to stop drinking, yet he refuses to submit himself into a treatment program or AA. Individuals with addiction problems have patterns in their lives that go beyond just the use of one particular substance. Thus, in this situation, this man is taking care of part of the problem, but leaving himself exposed to have other issues surface in his life.

When people deal with the majority of the problem, they mistakenly believe that they are on track with their goals. By doing 90 percent of what they need to do, they think they are out of the woods. The truth is, a person can be 90 percent right, but 100 percent wrong.

Denying a key piece of information can really throw off the expected results. If a person attempted to solve a math problem with only 90 percent of the numbers, the answer would be 100 percent wrong. If the answer is supposed to be 10, but the result is 9, isn't the answer 100 percent wrong?

Sometimes the missing piece of the equation is in the application of the information. An individual can speak truth, but be ineffective in presentation. I have seen many people come across so hard in their positions it is like they attempt to beat people into submission with a truth stick. The content of their information is 90 percent of their presentation, but the remaining 10 percent of their delivery makes the whole interaction backfire. I remember specifically when a man brought his twenty-something daughter with him to meet with me. He was a moral and honest man who absolutely believed in the presence of right and wrong. I listened to him describe the things that his daughter was doing and how they could have a negative impact on her life. Specifically, she was spending time with a married man who was much older. I also listened to his accounting of how he intervened in her life by letting himself in her home and kicking this man out of her house. After I listened to all the things he said, I told him, "You are right on every point you made. Every concern you have about your daughter is valid. However, you can be right about everything, yet still be wrong in how you approached the situation." I explained that the more he inserted his control in his adult daughter's life, the more he is risking harming their relationship, and if anything she will be more likely to lock herself into bad decisions. I suggested that he needed to trust in the fact that he and his wife raised her with a good foundation of morals and values, which she will settle back down upon as she matures. This man has great intentions, but his approach will work against his goals, which are for his daughter to make better choices. Not only did he need to understand the right answers, he also needed to recognize that a large percentage of success is related to being effective with those right answers.

Many things in life are easy to learn, but impossible to master.

It's not that we have to do everything perfectly before we can be successful. If this were the case, nobody would ever be successful. We just have to be willing to admit the fact that we don't have all the answers and there are blind spots when we examine our own lives. The only way to keep on track in life is to recognize that even when we are on a good path towards our goals, we still need to be open to the last 10 percent that we need to change. We need to understand that many things in life are easy to learn, but impossible to master. Many successful people will report that the more they learn in their field, the more they come to a realization of how much they really don't know. As long as we continue to embrace humility based on the fact that we will never arrive, we will be able to accomplish greater results in our lives than we ever imagined.

The truth will set you free

Once we break through our self-imposed lies and admit that we are lost, we must then try and figure out just how lost we really are. Sometimes the starting point is something that we don't want to face. We don't want to admit that we are that far off or have so far to go. It is almost as if we will feel like we are going backwards if we admit where we are. We cover our ears with our hands and say "la la la" repeatedly in hopes to drown out the truth. It is the same type of logic that says, "If I don't go to the doctor, I won't find out that this lump on my chest is cancer. I don't want to have cancer. This way, I won't have to deal with it." Clearly, not facing that you might have cancer won't make cancer go away. In fact, delaying it will only exacerbate the problem if it needs to be addressed.

Opening up and facing issues completely in our life is a freeing experience. In the Bible (John 8:32), Jesus tells us that the truth will set us free. The corollary to this statement is that a lie will hold us in bondage. This is especially true when we attempt to lie to ourselves.

I mentored a man named Bob over a period of a couple years. The first time I met Bob; he was arrogant, controlling, and completely self-centered. Not many people challenge my credentials and religious education before they agree to listen to what I have to say. I remember thinking to myself, "Great, I don't get paid enough for this."

The truth will set us free–a lie will hold us in bondage.

Bob was in his early thirties, married to a beautiful woman and had a couple of small children. He was very successful in business and was about to sell a start-up company for over a million dollars. Although Bob had seemingly good business building skills, many other areas in his life were a mess. And honestly, the truth is that if Bob applied solid principles in the development of his business, he could have grown it to ten million dollars instead of only one. His approach to life placed a serious governor switch on his potential success. I once told Bob that he was only operating at seventy percent of his potential. When I told him this, it was like a freight train ran over him. He looked at me and said, "Another business mentor in my life told me the same thing." I believe that hearing it twice somehow allowed it to get through to him.

Bob knew that he had a strong drive to succeed, but he didn't connect his high level of motivation to underlying fear. He had spent his life trying to overcome his insecurities by being the best at everything. He won at everything he did, at any cost. Bob openly admitted to using other people to achieve what he wanted in life. And likewise, he was guarded so other people wouldn't use him. Bob didn't have any real friends, mostly because he wouldn't allow himself to be open and vulnerable. He was too focused on showing everybody up and beating them down.

Honestly, I would have predicted that Bob was so locked into his life perspective that he wouldn't change. That just goes to show you how unpredictable people really are. Whether someone decides to change or not is based on his or her own personal decision. Anybody can make the decision to change–no matter how long or how extreme they have been doing the wrong things. I have been reminded many times, by being wrong, to not attempt to determine who will or will not change based on how they present. I can't bring about change in others any more than I make our cat want to sit in my wife's lap (running joke in our family).

The first time I witnessed Bob break down in tears over the pain he had in his life, I saw hope. He had spent his entire life refusing to be vulnerable–for him to express it was huge. Over the next few months, Bob slowly allowed more and more humility into his life. He started to be less critical of his wife, and with other people in general. Bob began to intellectually understand our talks and slowly the truth worked its way into his heart.

Whether someone decides to change or not is based on his or her own personal decision.

At one point, Bob openly confessed to me, "I have been living in fear my entire life." I think he was expecting me to be shocked and say "Really?" He seemed to be taken aback when I told him "Good." I think Bob found it difficult to believe that he wasn't telling me anything I didn't already know.

Bob said that his parents had a moderate degree of success, yet they made most of their own decisions out of fear. He relayed that his parents were miserable and did not have good relationships with their own children. In a conversation with his dad, Bob saw his own thought process in his dad's fear-based logic, and it scared him. He realized that he was becoming his dad, but he didn't want his life to turn out the same way. It shook Bob to see himself so clearly in the reflection of his father. He said, "I don't want that, I have to stop living in fear."

I told Bob, "You get it, good for you." He looked at me confused and said, "I don't feel like I get it." I explained that he didn't have to know everything. The biggest step of all is recognizing that he is lost–that he is following a path that will lead him to a place he doesn't want to go. Once he got that, the rest is simply walking it out.

Several months passed by and Bob and I were talking about one of the guys that he mentors. Ironically, the guy sounded very similar to how Bob was when I first met him. Bob shared how this guy was successful, but just didn't see how his controlling behavior was holding him back from having a good marriage or even getting further in business. By this time, Bob could so clearly see how this guy was simply missing the much larger potential he had in his life because he was living in a self-imposed lie. Bob reflected on how this guy was a mirror image of him just a short time ago. This realization drove home the lesson for Bob in how facing uncomfortable truth in his own life contributed to significant growth.

Admitting that we are lost can be a very humbling experience. We will often go from a sense of feeling in control to feeling quite vulnerable. Many people, when they experience this, misinterpret their vulnerability for being weak or soft. The truth is, when we finally humble ourselves to admit that we are lost, that freedom brings much more legitimate strength and success into our lives. By admitting that we are lost, we take the first step to find our path to potential.

Take Away Discussion Questions

1. God tells us that a person without vision will perish. A person with a vision who is not heading toward that vision will also perish. What examples can you think of where this is evident in your life?

2. Many people travel around the same path over and over again, yet never getting any closer to the things they want out of life. What are some familiar patterns you can identify?

3. Are you achieving the goals that you want? If not, you can't find your way to your desires unless you are willing to admit that you are lost. You can't change unless you face the fact that change is necessary. What changes need to be made?

4. One of the biggest obstacles you will face is overcoming your human tendency to lie to yourself about where you are. Don't worry, everybody lies to themselves. What are some of the lies that you tell yourself?

5. I don't want you to be critical of your own life. I'm not suggesting that you evaluate your path just so you can beat yourself up about not being where you want to be. The truth is designed to set you free. How could this work for you?

6. Isn't it better to realize that you are fifty miles off your goal and start being productive in the pursuit of it, than it is to lie to yourself that you are only two blocks from your goal and circle forever? Where have you been circling around your goals?

7. Don't negotiate around 10 percent of your life and convince yourself that 90 percent is good enough. You could end up frustrating yourself for a long time by not being willing to be completely open. What is one area where you have been unwilling to face the need for change?

8. Iron doesn't get sharpened by a marshmallow, and neither do people. Examine your associations. Do the people you choose to have in your life sharpen you towards growth, or allow you to stay lost?

9. God promises you that the truth will set you free. The truth is often quite difficult to accept, but once you accept truth in your life, you can finally begin your journey. What truths have you been avoiding?

10. Thomas Edison once stated, "A well defined problem is 90 percent solved." This statement clearly shows that most of the struggle is being honest with the issues. Spend some time defining your problems with a critical eye so you can begin your journey.

11. What is the one thing you are going to take away from this chapter and put into practice in your life, starting now?

Chapter 9

Your Emotions Are Not Your Friends
The Principle of Rational Decision

*You can't depend on your eyes when your
imagination is out of focus*

—*Mark Twain*

As a psychologist in the Air Force, I had the opportunity
to engage in many interesting experiences, such as evaluating
human factors related to flight and the study of aircraft
mishaps. I once had the chance to pilot an F-16 fighter jet
simulator. There is no question that such adventures were the
coolest parts of my job. This particular simulator is unique
because it is connected to a centrifuge in a large building,
which allows the pilot to experience g-forces.

When I sat in the cockpit and the hatch closed down
around me, I found myself surrounded by video screens that
provided a realistic virtual-reality of a runway nestled between
a breathtaking mountain range. The controls of the simulator
were identical of those in an F-16 cockpit. An Airman sitting
in a control booth spoke to me through my headset. He
provided a quick overview of our flight-plan and then gave
me the okay to start taxiing and lift off. I powered up and my
virtual plane began to move down the runway. As I pulled

back on the stick I not only saw myself leaving the ground, I actually felt the plane climb. The g-force generated by the spinning centrifuge pressed my body into the seat as I climbed past five thousand feet.

I was still climbing and penetrating some cloud cover when my heart skipped a beat in reaction to all of the screens turning black, leaving me sitting in complete darkness. I could still feel the plane climbing when the voice came over the headset, "Captain Bennett, we're experiencing some technical difficulties, just try and level out the aircraft until we get the screens back on." I pushed forward on the stick and felt the weight of my body ease off the seat as I brought my aircraft back to what I determined to be level. I'm flying in the dark for only a few moments when the screens came back on and I realized that I am not level at all. My plane is flying about a twenty degrees negative attitude (pointing downward) and picking up more speed as I rocketed towards the ground. In a desperate attempt to recover the dive I pulled back on the stick as I noticed the altimeter register that I was only five hundred feet from the ground. In less time than it took to catch my breath, I watched my own death. Good thing it was virtual reality at that point.

I later realized that everything I experienced was part of the flight program. There were no technical difficulties–the blackout was a simulation to train pilots to not trust their feelings. Since human factors contribute to crashes, pilots must learn how the introduction of forces applied to their bodies will distort their feelings. This training is necessary for them to trust their instruments over their own intuition.

During the time I was sitting in the dark, I would have sworn based on my feelings that I was flying level. My feelings were wrong, but they sure seemed real to me. I would have probably continued to believe my feelings, if I had not seen with my own eyes the hard data of me crashing into the ground. The afternoon training I experienced made a huge impact in my understanding of how emotions can be misleading.

Emotions often do not take us to where we want to go.
Yet, if this is true why do we use them so much of the time?
The circular answer is, because they feel right. But of course
they feel right, we are the ones who are feeling them. When
we tell ourselves that we are on course, but we don't compare
that feeling to anything substantial, we are risking certain
failure. Unfortunately, many people don't recognize how far
off their emotions took them until they crash and burn.

Balanced is Best

When my sister Patty read the title of this chapter, she put
it down on the table and said that her emotions have been
quite valuable to her in her life. She asked if I am saying that
we shouldn't allow ourselves to feel things. Patty's comments
are somewhat typical, in that people often hear the truth of
principles as extreme statements.

Of course emotions are not evil–God gives us emotions
for a reason. When I say that our emotions are not our
friends, I am referring to the tendency for people to allow
their emotions to become out of balance.

Emotions will have a detrimental impact in our lives if
they are either under-expressed or over-expressed. In many
ways the healthy balance of emotions is much like a proper
control of fire. Feelings are not bad, anymore than fire is bad.
If we have no fire, we will be cold and possibly even die. Fire
within our control is beneficial to our survival, but left
unchecked, it will turn destructive. You see, the proper use
for fire is when we keep it within our discipline. We use fire
when fire serves a need. We must stay in control of the fire or
the fire will control us.

We all are designed to feel and it is not healthy if we turn
off our emotions and go through life like some sort of robot.
Unfortunately, some people have learned to cope with
difficult things in their lives by turning off their emotions.
Usually this occurs when they were children and faced
something painful. They learned in their youth that if they

don't allow themselves to feel, the hardships or abuse doesn't hurt as bad. Like most strategies we use to cope with challenges, losing one's emotional expression results in an ongoing struggle with their connection to others.

Randy is a guy who demonstrated a very difficult time connecting with his wife. This couple came to see me after his wife reached her frustration tolerance level in not getting her emotional needs met. Randy is in his mid-forties and showed the ability to express two emotional states: humor and anger.

Most of the time, Randy was unemotional about everything and tended to see other's emotional responses as weakness. In fact, he prided himself on his ability to be analytical about life. His wife wanted to feel some emotional intimacy, but Randy struggled meeting her there. When he felt uncomfortable, Randy mostly moved towards humor. He often joked about things that were sensitive and important to his wife, which led her to feel devalued and unloved.

When conflict finally broke into their marriage, his other emotion came to the surface and dominated the fight. When his humor was rejected because his wife felt like he didn't care, Randy escalated quickly through irritation and then anger. It is as if his emotional reaction got triggered, and he lost his prided analytical nature. Randy's volume elevated as he pointed out all the things he did to show his wife that he loved her. Through Randy's rants, he berated and dominated his wife as he accused her of wanting him to be overly sensitive like one of her girlfriends. This behavior put them into a tailspin that took several weeks in which to recover.

Come to find out, Randy grew up with a father who did not show any form of emotional warmth. Randy's father farmed most of his life after returning from World War II. His father treated him with a serious, distant, and critical attitude. Probably from his own upbringing and experiences, Randy's father disconnected and became emotional unavailable to those around him. Randy recalled that when he was just a boy, his father ridiculed him for crying when he hit his thumb with a hammer. It didn't take much time around his father for this young boy to shut off his emotions as a mechanism of survival. He learned to associate emotions with weakness from his father's example.

Randy realized that if he didn't feel anything, he couldn't get his feelings hurt. So, he ignored all of his emotions, except the two that allowed him to feel strong. With his humor, he was able to keep from going into vulnerable areas of his life. He simply joked his way out of dealing with things. His anger allowed him to feel strong again when he was faced with vulnerability.

Like the earlier example of fire, this man became so fearful of what would happen if he allowed his emotions to be present, that he never allowed the fire to be lit. Unfortunately, out of his fear of fire, he accumulated a large slash pile of life experiences and conflicts that grew to the point of becoming a fire hazard. Once something sparked into that pile, the whole thing just turned into a raging blaze, burning completely out of control. This man's unwillingness to feel clearly brought a very negative pattern into his life.

When emotions are used to direct everything we think or do, we place ourselves in a reactionary mode that ends up being very unproductive.

Fortunately, once Randy recognized that he extended the negative pattern from his father into his own marriage and family, he started to change. He saw that being analytical wasn't a sign of strength–it represented fear of vulnerability. This allowed Randy to start stretching out of his comfort zone and taking chances in the emotional relationship with his wife.

The opposite of Randy on this emotional continuum is the person who acts upon their feelings all the time. It is like they have a flamethrower that spews fire every direction it's pointed. When emotions are used to direct everything we think or do, we place ourselves in a reactionary mode that ends up being very unproductive.

Ted is the opposite of Randy when it came to his willingness to feel. Yet, surprisingly, Ted didn't do much better at meeting the emotional needs of his wife. Ted could emote, but his emotions controlled him. When Ted and Angie entered counseling, Angie expressed that she was questioning her willingness to stay in the marriage. Ted primarily reported feeling insecure and constant fear that Angie was doing nothing more than strategizing her exit from him. Even though they both committed to counseling, Ted constantly badgered Angie throughout the week regarding her desire to continue with the marriage. I explained repeatedly to Ted that his need to question Angie was an emotional reaction based in his insecurity of the relationship. I validated his feelings of insecurity because they are normal based on the difficult situation. However, I explained that the action of him expressing those feelings was not in his best interests. Every time he gave into that emotion and uttered those words, he drove his wife further away. Angie confirmed this dynamic. She said that she actually felt her skin crawl and noticed how she pulled back even further from Ted each time he wanted to talk about their future together.

Sometimes individuals need the opportunity to fail more than anything else.

You see, Ted had the feelings of insecurity, but since he didn't manage the expression of those feelings and thus let them run wild, he created situations in his life that were opposite of what he wanted. As he drove Angie away, he experienced greater levels of insecurity. Ted's fire just kept burning more and more out of control in a vicious cycle.

Keep in mind, Ted attempted to make his situation better. He felt that checking in with his wife to get confirmation of their relationship would help his insecurity go away. The problem is, because he gave into his emotion, his marriage got worse, and he moved further from his goal.

Clearly, these negative types of emotions, such as frustration, irritation, insecurity, or anger are not good to let go wild, but what about feelings that we tend to think of as positive? Honestly, the same principle applies whether we are talking about acting out of our positive or negative feelings.

An emotion of compassion towards somebody else would be considered a "good feeling." I'm personally glad that we, as human beings, feel compassion for one another. But, even with such an honorable feeling, we have to be careful how we choose to respond to it. If we give in to our feelings of compassion too much it can become unbalanced and unhealthy. Compassion taken to an extreme turns into a pattern of enabling others because we are constantly giving things to them. When someone is given everything they want they stop taking personal responsibility for their own life. It is a difficult balance to have compassion for people and not give them what they want, but rather give them what they need. Sometimes individuals need the opportunity to fail more than anything else. This means that having compassion for them might look like doing nothing.

It can be quite difficult to override the actions associated with positive feelings because they seem like the right and loving things to do. This was evident with a single mom I spoke to. She had three children, the youngest of whom was an adolescent daughter diagnosed with cancer around the age of nine. Clearly this is a horrible situation. I thank God that all my boys are healthy and I have never had to deal with such adversity. Who wouldn't have compassion for an innocent child with such an affliction? Yet, this mom responded to her daughter too frequently based on her emotion of compassion. Her resulting attitudes and behavior was a focused attempt to make her daughter's life easier.

"What's wrong with that?" you might ask. "Her daughter had a bad situation, why shouldn't her mom make her life easy?"

Because, her daughter stopped trying to make her own life better. Her daughter started to identify with the role of helpless victim and expected others to serve her. As she got older, she burnt relationships because people got tired of her "poor me" mentality. When individuals attempted to hold this girl accountable for self-care behaviors, for which she was clearly capable, she promoted the "I'm a sick child" role. So, what happens to this "sick child" if she recovers from cancer and becomes a healthy adult? She will have to overcome some serious righteous selfishness that has been spoon-fed to her for years. Believing that she is incapable of caring for herself has not served this young woman well at all, yet this identity was formed out of the spirit of compassion of a loving mother.

God gives us the ability to feel because this is what connects us to others. Feelings pull on our heart and can even help us discover areas of insight. These emotions serve an important role, but we are served best when we use our emotions from a position of balance. If we either limit or over-express our emotions, they start to work against our best interests.

Feelings are not a good guide to truth

Wouldn't it be nice if we had an internal process that always led us to the right answer? We could just feel the correct response and be successful. Ever watch one of those action films where the hero fights several people at the same time? Punching one person as he is ducking an oncoming blow from behind. That type of movie is portraying this fighter as having an intuition that allows him to respond without having to think about what is happening. Imagine if you could go through life with such correct automatic reactions. No matter what problem came your way, you could just respond out of your emotions to achieve the results you want.

Our emotions do, in fact, influence and guide our actions. People don't like to admit it, but many of their decisions have a strong emotional component. Cars are bought, not for the bottom line of what one can afford or for potential investment, but based on how the leather feels or the aerodynamic lines of the design. Conflicts with others are escalated, not because it is in anybody's best interests, but because what the other person said or did triggered them. Emotions do contribute to our responses, just not always towards the best results.

People fall all along the continuum of emotional reactions. At one end you see people who are so emotional in their processing of information that they shift their course in life like a dog chasing chickens. They allow their emotions to rule them, so they lack the consistency and follow-through necessary to lead them to their goals. On the other end of this dynamic are people who tend to be quite unemotional. Their Spock-like quality results in taking them to more of a deliberate and thought-based course of action.

People find evidence of what they expect to see.

Regardless of how emotionally expressive individuals are, or aren't, they allow their emotions to influence them in a significant way.

Even the most intelligent and logical scientists will unintentionally bias the results of studies if they know too much about data. For example, in pharmaceutical research, studies are designed with a protocol called "double blind," which means that neither the subjects, nor the researchers have information about which drugs administered are "active." Studies are set up this way because if either the participants or the researches know which drugs are supposed to work, this knowledge taints the results. Most often, people find evidence of what they expect to see. Thus, nobody is free from the influence of his or her own emotions.

Across the board, people give way too much credibility to their emotions as guide to truth. They feel that something is right and then proceed based on their feelings. We keep doing this because we misinterpret our results. When our feelings are right, we give the credit to that gut reaction. "I caught him in a lie. I just knew that he wasn't telling me the truth." When our intuition does not pan out to be true, however, we still give credit to those feelings. "I can't prove it, but I know he is not telling the whole truth about what happened." So, we tend to embrace our feelings when they prove to be right, and make excuses when confirmation is not present. This "biased data collection" gives us the impression that our feelings are much more reliable than they really are.

"Wait Todd, I have great intuition about people. Are you saying that my feelings are wrong when I have lots of evidence that they are right?"

Friends, please understand that your feelings don't measure right vs. wrong, good vs. bad, or true vs. untrue. It would be great if this were the case because you could easily do all the correct things with such an internal compass. Unfortunately, this is not how it works. Your feelings can lead you to what is right, good, and true, but this will happen only when these results have been consistent in your life. You see, your feelings measure one thing: familiar vs. unfamiliar.

If you have great intuition in an area of life, there is a good chance that you are successful there. For you in that area, those good results are familiar and thus your feelings simply line you up for more and more successes. For example, if you have a knack for business and a track record for demonstrating consistent growth in sales, you will likely be able to listen to proposals and experience a feeling for whether the idea will work or not. Or if you deal with a great number of people in your job, you might be able to have accurate impressions of new people you meet. The truth is, if your feelings align with existing good decisions, you will probably make the correct call using your intuition.

Do not be fooled, however, to believe that your strengths and corresponding feelings in one area of your life automatically define your emotions as reliable in all areas. Just because you can manage a large company into sustainable growth does not mean your parenting is effective, even if it does feel right. Simply because you have social intuition, don't fall into the trap of thinking you know what your spouse is feeling. Nobody is strong in all areas of life and your emotions will, therefore, be accurate only some of the time.

"So, how do I discern when to pay attention to my gut?"

If you are already successful in something, follow your instinct, within reason. Your feelings in that situation will likely lead you to more success. If you are struggling in an area, stop listening to your emotional reasoning. In this case, your feelings are not your friends. The only thing your feelings will do is keep you making the same decisions. You might not like the decisions you make or the results of those decisions, but believe it or not, you have a degree of comfort associated with that path. A person can dislike something in their life, yet be very familiar with it.

There is a woman named Megan in her early thirties who had a rough upbringing. Megan grew up in a family of nudists and was exposed to sexual abuse and various other poor boundaries. Megan once described an event in her life that happened around the age of fourteen. She reported that she got out of the shower and her father was standing naked, shaving at the sink. When questioned about what feelings were present at the time, Megan said, "It was just normal—something that happened all the time. I didn't think anything of it." Megan didn't realize that what she went through was bad until much later in her life when she learned that her family wasn't "normal." What she experienced was familiar to her, therefore, Megan's feelings didn't communicate to her that it was wrong.

Keep in mind, when people have some level of familiarity with a negative situation, this does not mean that they choose the consequences that come with that path. Familiar does not equate to desire. Just because a woman who grew up with a controlling father might very likely find herself in relationships with controlling men, this doesn't mean that she wants to be dominated. Just because a man grew up in the same family and tends to control women, it doesn't mean that

he wants a string of unhealthy relationships. People follow
familiar paths because it is what they know, not because it's
what they seek.

"Why would someone continue to follow their feelings
when they don't get positive results?"

People follow their feelings and engage in non-productive
and even destructive behaviors because the way they respond
is normal to them and they tell themselves that it should
work. I remember counseling a man named Jeff who married
a very sweet woman who had a son from a prior relationship.
Jeff had no children of his own, but he had lots of ideas what
parents and kids should do. Jeff tended to be an analytical
type of person who liked things organized and structured. He
approached his stepson, who was about twelve at the time,
with the perspective of building his character and integrity.
Jeff had a lot of rules and tended to be critical and suspicious
of his stepson. I likened his parenting to more of a military
environment than a loving and structured home.

Jeff's approach to his stepson created a huge amount of
conflict between him and his wife. The more Jeff got critical
of this boy, the more his wife became protective and didn't
address real issues with her son.

The problems related to Jeff and his stepson seemed to be
raised in counseling for over a solid year. Perspective was
given to Jeff about why his critical and authoritarian approach
wouldn't work. Jeff acted like he listened, but the information
shared with him was too far opposite of what felt was right.
So, he attempted to implement the correct parenting
perspective, but continually reverted back to his old ways.
Thus, he never really changed. As a result, his relationship
with his stepson continued to get worse and worse.

Jeff never seemed to grasp the concept that the things he
was doing simply didn't produce results. I attempted to
explain to Jeff that if he were an orchard farmer, his success
would be based on his demonstrated ability to produce fruit.
(All results from our behaviors can be evaluated the same
way.) Jeff didn't like hearing that he didn't have any

parenting fruit in his life. All his philosophy regarding parenting was just that–philosophy, with no experience or results. Jeff only had his emotions from which to operate, and since those feelings told him his interventions should work, he believed he was right.

Jeff was just simply not willing to apply a different strategy in his life that went against his feelings. Thus, his feelings kept him doing a very unproductive, yet familiar, behavior cycle. Jeff didn't want the results of ongoing conflict his family. He did not desire a strained relationship with his wife or for his stepson to hate him. He didn't want his wife to divorce him and have yet another failed relationship under his belt. But all of that is what happened. Jeff had wanted a happy family, to be loved and respected, and even for his stepson to grow up to be a good and honorable man. But Jeff's intentions were never realized because he didn't change his response from what seemed right to him.

The problem is, our feelings seem so real. I have even heard people say that their feelings regarding an issue were so powerful that they attributed them to God's communication. It is difficult to argue with this logic without sounding like a doubting or non-spiritual person. My take on this, however, is that God does communicate with us. But why would God choose to communicate to us through an emotional channel, when our emotions are so unreliable? Is that the voice of God, fear, or desire that you feel? It is difficult to tell. I believe that since our emotions are based on familiarity, using the statement of "God's will" is a good way to justify doing what our emotions want us to do.

True strength comes from when we choose to act in what is right instead of what feels right.

Any person can easily make decisions that are consistent with their emotions. This does not take any strength or self-discipline at all. True strength comes from when we choose to act in what is right instead of what feels right.

Once you accept the truth that your feelings relate only to familiarity, apply that knowledge to areas in your life that need attention. You can evaluate where you need to go against your feelings by determining where your fruit trees don't produce. If you do not have the success you desire in some area of your life, be willing to change. You need to realize that if you follow your feelings in non-productive areas of your life, you will never have success there. Your feelings align with familiarity, and unfortunately in some areas your familiar experience is failure. Thus, giving into what seems normal and natural will keep you stuck in a vicious cycle that prevents you from achieving the successes you desire.

Honestly, most of the time the right thing to do is probably the opposite of what you feel like doing. Therefore, we have to constantly check our motives for why we choose to do the things we do. Our feelings, by themselves, are not a good way to check our course because they simply take us down familiar paths.

Feelings are a thermometer

As I stood there looking in the mirror, I realized that I was not happy with the thirty or so extra pounds that I was carrying. It seemed like when I was in my teens and twenties, I could have four plates of food at a buffet and never even consider gaining weight. When I hit my thirties, however, I no longer experienced that blessing. I didn't like the extra weight, but I don't tend to be a very obsessive guy, so I didn't feel an internal pressure to do anything about it. I knew that I needed to eat better and exercise, but… "Today doesn't seem like a good day to start. The weather is too cold to run, the traffic is too heavy to ride my bike, and the desserts are too good to pass up. I will start watching my weight when I feel like it, I will start exercising when I have the extra energy, and I will discipline myself when it doesn't seem so hard." I don't even have to tell you that those attitudes didn't lead to a change.

I have listened to many people say that they will change when it is a better time, or when things in their lives have calmed down. Please hear me, if you wait to act differently until you feel like it, you will be waiting forever. If you want change in your life, you will need to change your thoughts and actions before you have the feelings to support it. We will never change our feelings before we change our attitudes and behaviors. Our feelings do not come first.

You have to think and act in ways that are consistent with what you want, not what you already feel. Remember, your feelings connect you to familiarity–if you act according to your feelings your thoughts and behaviors will be no different than what you've already carried out in the past. Albert Einstein defined insanity by doing the same things and expecting different results. If you don't change what you do or think, you won't change.

If you don't change what you do or think, you won't change.

The problem for most people is that change is different and brings about feelings of uneasiness, awkwardness, insecurity, and vulnerability. People don't like feeling these things because they are uncomfortable. As pointed out above, we like to feel the familiar, even if it leads to negative results. Unfortunately, a comfort zone is a failure zone.

Many people want change to enter into their lives, and they are waiting for opportunity to knock. They want things to be different, but they don't feel inspired to make things happen. They are foolishly wishing for opportunity to knock down the door and roust them into success. If we are not willing to leave the comfort of our La-Z-Boy to make different things happen, opportunity simply passes by.

It is important to break out of the cycle of operating off of your feelings. If you want to change your emotions, you need to understand that feelings don't change on their own–you will not experience a surge of energy that will propel you towards different results. Your feelings are nothing more than a passive measuring device of your thoughts, actions, beliefs, habits, experience, and ultimately character.

The difference between an active and a passive process is similar to what distinguishes a thermostat from a thermometer. A thermometer does nothing but report how hot or cold an environment is. It doesn't determine what is comfortable, correct, or even communicate something's potential. A thermometer only reports the data that is present. For example, if your house is sixty degrees Fahrenheit, a thermometer just tells you the temperature–it doesn't speak to the way it should be, or provide you a process to change. In a sixty degree environment you would probably be cold, but it would be silly for you to look at the thermometer and say, "Well, I guess I am supposed to be cold, it must be the way God made it to be." Nor do we stand at the thermometer and tap it in the hopes that if it changes we will feel warmer.

If we are cold in a sixty-degree home, the correct response is to go to the thermostat and turn up the furnace to a comfortable seventy degrees. Once the thermostat is set at seventy, it slowly changes the environment, which is registered on the thermometer. Eventually, our thermometer will report what we want it to be.

If our feelings were like a thermometer, our thermostat would be our thoughts and actions. If we only have thoughts and actions that are consistent with our emotions, we will never change. This is like being cold in a sixty-degree home, but leaving the thermostat set at sixty because it is consistent with how we feel.

A real life example would be if you feel depressed, then dwell on how bad things are and stay in bed all day long, your negative feelings will tend to stay the same. Or if you have anxiety or fears and you avoid those things, your thoughts and behaviors will make those fears stronger.

If we are ever in a position where our thoughts, actions, feelings, values, and circumstances don't line up, we feel uneasy. We will tend to make every effort to bring them all into agreement. This is where we engage in rationalization or even delusion. If we feel something, we will tend to find a way to make it work, even if it is to develop our own facts. I'm sure you are saying, "I don't do that." Yes you do. Everybody does to a degree–it's called interpretation and justification. You would probably be surprised how many of your interpretations you categorize as facts to justify your feelings.

Homeostasis is where things change to match up and develop equilibrium. If you pour water on the counter it will be even across the puddle. The entire universe tends to gravitate towards homeostasis, so it is normal that you do too. If you have a negative attitude about something, your actions have to match to keep that balance. This creates a reoccurring cycle that, without intervention, won't likely change.

So the key is to break out of your homeostasis and not keep your thoughts and actions in line with feelings that don't work. If you are feeling negative about yourself, but you tell yourself that you are valuable, it will feel like a lie. If you feel a lack of energy but put on your shoes and go for a walk, you might ask yourself "Why am I doing this?" This is because you are disrupting a natural pull for homeostasis.

If you are like many of the people who have heard this information, you might say, "But if I say or do something that I don't feel, that's like I am lying to myself or playing some type of game that isn't real." I will admit to you that this can seem artificial because when you do things that go against your feelings it does feel awkward, vulnerable, or deceptive. When you act against your feelings it is not manipulation or a game, you are breaking a cycle.

Thinking or doing something opposite your feelings is just like when you turn that thermostat to seventy degrees, but the thermometer continues to read sixty degrees for some time. You simply recognize that it takes time for the furnace to warm the home and change the feeling. Likewise, when you change your thoughts or actions, it will seem inconsistent with your feelings for a while–at least until those new beliefs and behaviors have a chance to bring about change.

It is very important to realize that God gave each and every one of us emotions for a reason. Emotions are very useful for us when we keep them in a healthy balance and do not allow the presence or absence of them to control our lives. We must also recognize that our intuition is not an accurate guide to truth, only to what is familiar to us. If we have successful areas, the correct behaviors will be almost instinctual. However, if we don't have fruit on our trees, it is important to stop justifying what should work and change to what does work? Finally, it is critical to understand how to change our feelings. We bring about change in our feelings by changing our thoughts and behaviors, not the other way around. Getting out of our comfort zones is never easy, but always necessary if we want different results down the line.

Take Away Discussion Questions

1. People fall somewhere on a continuum of emotional expression. Some wear their hearts on their sleeve, but others are much more analytical. Where do you believe you are on this line?

2. If we don't keep our emotions in check they can control us and even destroy us. What is an example of where you allowed your feelings to take charge of you?

3. To use your feelings successfully, you have to take charge of them. How do think this is done without getting out of balance in the other direction?

4. You must be purposeful and productive in allowing your feelings to lead you where you want to go. The only way to do this is to trust your feelings in situations where you have demonstrated the proper fruit. What are some of these areas in your life?

5. Your feelings are not based in truth–they are based in familiarity. What are some examples of this?

6. Your feeling of being ready to do something will come secondary to the decision and action components that are consistent with what you want out of life. What is an example of where you have waited for change to happen?

7. Fear of the unknown is one of the greatest fears of mankind. If you fail to act because of fear, you are significantly blocking your potential for greatness. What have been some of your fears that have kept you from moving forward?

8. Fear has been defined as False Expectations Appearing Real. Based on this definition, the best way to eliminate fears in life is to attack them head on. Why do you suppose this works?

9. Do not allow yourself to be controlled by your fear–use it as a source of motivation in your life. What would happen if you wait to be less fearful before you act?

10. Your feelings can only be your friends if you understand the limitations of them and you chose to stay in charge of your own life. What changes are you going to make to try and achieve this for your future?

11. What is the one thing you are going to take away from this chapter and put into practice in your life, starting now?

Chapter 10

The Answer is Found in the Mirror
The Principle of Personal Responsibility

> *I believe that every right implies a responsibility;*
> *every opportunity, an obligation; every possession, a*
> *duty.*
>
> — *John D. Rockefeller*
>
> *The price of greatness is responsibility.*
>
> — *Winston Churchill*

I first interviewed Rachel several years ago. Rachel fit the profile of the classic drug addict. She lived a self-focused life and justified every minute of it. She constantly minimized her drug use and even denied charges filed against her for possession. She argued that she was unjustly arrested because the drugs found in her home belonged to somebody else. Needless to say, there were many ongoing consequences that occurred in Rachel's life. She was evicted from multiple homes, lost all jobs, and destroyed relationships. Even Rachel's three children expressed bitter anger at her.

The first time I spoke with Rachel, she identified herself as a victim. She was a victim of her drug use, a victim of bad parents, a victim of living on the wrong side of town, and a victim by how other people used her.

Rachel saw the consequences in her life as things other people did to her. She believed that her kids didn't want anything to do with her because their father poisoned them against her. Rachel wanted a relationship with her kids, but she didn't take responsibility for the reason things were so bad. Based on how she was constantly shifting the blame for her consequences, it was fairly easy to predict that Rachel was at risk of not changing her patterns in life.

Even though Rachel said she was never going to use drugs again for her kids' sake, she was actually setting herself up to fail. Saying that she was going to change when she didn't accept personal responsibility for her situation meant that she wasn't going to address the real issues. In fact, not long after she started seeing her kids again, Rachel fell back into her drug habit. Back to jail she went, and she hit bottom harder than she ever had.

One of the benefits of Rachel going back to jail occurred when she decided to honestly change her life. She started this change process by taking responsibility for the mess she had created.

By the time I interviewed Rachael a second time a couple years had passed. Rachel had spent a good amount of time in jail and continued to be involved in an outpatient drug treatment program upon her release. Many people talk about how they changed in jail, when most of them actually didn't– but there was something different about Rachel. Her attitude had completely shifted.

Rachel no longer looked to outside explanations for the consequences she endured. Even when it came to her children's anger and resentment of her, she identified that she caused it by her lack of stability in their lives.

Rachel also developed some pretty good insight regarding the onset of her blame shifting. She identified that her parents never held her accountable for anything in her life. Rachel said that when she was caught with marijuana in high school, her parents made the charges go away. Every time she had negative consequences from her poor choices, her parents handed her excuses on a silver platter. When she used her rent money to buy drugs, her parents stepped in and kept her from being kicked out on the street. Rachel realized that she was led to believe that she wasn't responsible for the bad things that happened to her. This belief, however, kept her in a negative and non-productive pattern. Although having something or somebody to blame for all the bad things in her life probably felt better than looking in the mirror, such a perspective kept her from breaking out of her cycle and changing her life.

Looking in the mirror is the starting place to change. It is never a great feeling to bring the reasons for our consequences back onto our own shoulders. Some people never do. But there is also a freedom that comes with looking in the mirror because nobody but you has the ability to change your circumstances.

Being a victim is a state of mind

A long time ago there weren't so many regulations on research studies. As a result psychologists sometimes even used torture to evaluate their hypotheses. In one particular study researchers placed a dog in a cage with an electric grid on the floor. The evaluators conducted multiple trials of sending pulses of non-deadly, yet painful shock throughout the floor. The poor dog initially yelped and frantically ran around the cage in an attempt to escape. After many series of shocks without any success of avoiding it, the dog quit trying to escape and curled up in the corner of the cage.

An interesting thing happened at this point in the experiment. The researchers opened up the door to the cage and applied another surge of electricity to the floor. One would think that the dog would seize the opportunity and run for its life, but the dog did nothing. The animal had seemingly given up trying to escape and just accepted the negative circumstance. The dog had supposedly learned that it was truly helpless. The researchers termed the dog's behavioral response as "learned helplessness" and applied it to human nature as well.

Human beings are not often tortured by being placed in an electrified cage, but they undergo other forms of abuse, victimization, or negative circumstance. Such traumas can encompass a wide range of experiences for individuals. Abuse can be sexual, physical, verbal, or emotional. People can feel victimized by traumatic events in their childhoods, such as death or parental divorce. Negative circumstances can be issues like poverty, bigotry, or personal challenges. Sometimes people even see themselves as victimized by their own actions. They might attempt to change something in their life, but fail repeatedly.

If you have experienced abuse in your life, I am honestly sorry. Nobody should have to experience abuse. When a child has been treated as if they have no value, that self-image can persist throughout his or her life. It is sad to see the pain that people can carry for years.

There is a significant difference between being victimized and being a victim. If you or someone you know experienced abuse or trauma, such as the examples above, this is victimization. Anybody could be, and unfortunately too many people are, victimized. Let's face the disconcerting facts–the world can be a nasty place and bad things happen to even the most innocent people. Victimizations are events or series of events that happen to individuals and are circumstances beyond their control.

Victimization is not a state of mind, but being a victim is. We move from "victimization" to "victim" when we allow something that happens to us to define who we are. Being a victim is a self-image, not a circumstance. Having a victim state of mind is like the dog that has an open door to change its situation, yet convinces itself that nothing can be done.

There are several problems with developing a victim self-image. Sometimes, people with this identity will convince themselves that they deserve the negative consequences they have in life. Also, such persons will often make one bad decision after another that continually places them in a position to experience ongoing victimization. The biggest problem, however, is that when individuals see themselves as a victim, they don't look in the mirror to change their situation.

Individuals are natural data collectors–they go through life evaluating their experiences and then use this information to assign their own value and predict their future. When people are abused or victimized, they often internalize these behaviors as something about them. One could explain this by understanding our inherent

Being a victim is a self-image, not a circumstance.

egocentric nature of making everything about us. When bad things happen to us, we tend to evaluate that negative based on who we are. Children often interpret issues such as their parents divorce as "Why am I so unlovable that my daddy doesn't want to live with me anymore?" Individuals often carry these negative self-blame and victim processes into their adult lives and continue to expect bad things to happen.

Not only do people with a victim state of mind expect negative results out of life, they make this an active process. In the previous chapter on emotions, we discussed how feelings lead us into familiar situations–this is especially true with a victim mentality. Individuals who identify with their victimization tend to place themselves in one situation after another where victimization is likely. A woman who has a history of physical abuse will often find herself in abusive relationships. A man who felt controlled by his mother will tend to marry a dominant and controlling woman.

When people see themselves as a victim, they accept a passive response style to life. They think that the things that happen to them are out of their control, much like what they experienced in childhood. The truth is, however, that individuals have much more control over their current life that they sometimes allow themselves to believe.

When individuals look everyplace else but the mirror, they are waiting passively for something to happen for change to take place. The more people tend to see themselves as being a victim, the more they respond with eerily similarity to those poor dogs from the study–they quit trying to do something to make their life better.

Nobody is as vested in changing your situation than you. Plus, nobody has the ability to change the course of your life other than you. Be careful to not allow things outside of your control to dictate your lack of success in your life. You have been given unique abilities and everything you need to break out of the chains that you believe limit your accomplishments.

We need to get to the point where we shift our focus from the negative of our families, to redefining how we want our children and our grandchildren to see us.

Nobody is as vested in changing your situation than you.

If we allow ourselves to blame our parents or grandparents for where we are in life, we will never break out of that cycle. Abraham Lincoln said it this way, "I don't know who my grandfather was; I am much more concerned to know what his grandson will be." Abraham Lincoln came from a poor and uneducated family background. His life was filled with hardship. Yet he continued to define himself through his own decisions based on principles that he held firmly in his heart. Even if Lincoln didn't like somebody, he took responsibility for that. He was once quoted in saying, "I don't like that man. I must get to know him better." That is an attitude of looking in the mirror.

A woman once pointed out to me, "Not everybody has the same opportunities in life. Some people are just born with disadvantages. That is why we have government programs, to help people when they can't help themselves."

It is true that not everybody is born with the same advantages. There are individuals who literally cannot care for themselves and we, as a human race, do have a moral obligation to care for each other. But there are many people who believe they need to be cared for, when in fact they are capable of providing for their own life. I realize that it sounds harsh to allow somebody the opportunity to fail, but it is harsher to interfere with his or her opportunity to succeed. But nobody should be stripped of the opportunity to take care of him or herself. Nobody else can solve a person's problems for them. When organizations attempt to solve the problems of individuals, things typically get worse. What starts off as a good and humane idea, tends to have more long-range negative outcomes.

For example, when a government program gives families income because of a legitimate need, those individuals are getting rewards without the necessary sacrifice and work. Getting something for nothing is very attractive and even addictive to most all individuals, just look at the amount of money people spend on lotteries and gambling. The problem is, when we get something without effort and sacrifice, we start to gravitate towards that easy path. The easy path will always take us away from the right path. In this case, if the subsistence continues on for very long, a person will stop looking to their own capabilities to accomplish things in their own life, and they will become dependent on others. This dependency strips individuals of their sense of self-worth and value. They actually begin to believe that they cannot survive without help or support. Thus, they stop dreaming, setting goals, and ultimately they stop growing. They become stagnant, living a life of mediocrity. Thus, what was intended to help actually hurts because it stripped the individual from their need to grow.

This is what makes America great. Not the size of government or the number of programs, but the longstanding position of our forefathers of individual freedom. It was written in our Declaration of Independence that among the inalienable rights of mankind, every person has the right to life, liberty, and the pursuit of happiness. Notice that our forefathers didn't say that everybody is guaranteed happiness, or that the government has the job to provide people with happiness or even an easier life. Our government was designed to simply provide the freedom for individuals to achieve their own goals, to take control of their own lives. As long as one person's pursuit of happiness doesn't infringe on the rights of another, our freedom in this country allows us to achieve our own dreams.

It's the classic adage, "Give a person a fish, you feed them for a day; teach a person to fish, you feed them for a lifetime." To follow this idea: "Develop a program of giving a person fish; they lose the desire and belief that they can fish for themselves. If you ever stop giving away fish, that person will starve."

If you look to a government program to solve problems, you will be on the lookout for a long time. Have you noticed that as our government has gotten bigger and bigger, it tends to generate more problems than it fixes? Have you noticed that many people in government positions can't even seem

The easy path will always take us away from the right path.

to manage their own lives or marriages effectively? Infidelity and illegal activity is almost so common in our government that we hardly pay attention to it anymore. Government officials need to understand that their private lives do relate to their public service. It is impossible to separate these things out–remember character is not contextual. How are people and organizations that cannot manage themselves ever going to solve your problems? Well, simply put, they're not.

Don't use God as an excuse to fail

Many people don't look to the mirror because of their religious convictions. They believe that God will give them everything they need in life.

I remember an experience of riding in the back seat of a Suburban, traveling towards the capitol Riyadh with several other Air Force medical officers stationed in Saudi Arabia. We were on a four-lane highway with at least six lanes of traffic and traveling at least seventy-five miles per hour to keep up with the traffic flow, but cars and trucks were passing us on both sides, going both directions. There is nothing like having two vehicles traveling over eighty miles per hour, coming directly at you, only to pass you on opposite sides of your car. Anybody who knows me knows that I have a control issue with driving to begin with–I don't even like being a passenger in a car when people are following the rules of the road. This ninety-minute road trip in Saudi Arabia was one of the longest rides I have ever been on.

Early in the trip, as I was cringing in the back seat, I asked the driver "Why is there so much chaos on the road?" He said that the Saudi's are Muslim and they drive with the underlying belief of Islam, which is "The will of Allah." Simply translated, they don't follow any rules–if they make it to their destination alive, it was the will of Allah. If they die, it was the will of Allah. I thought to myself, "What about personal responsibility for good and safe choices? If they kill all of us because they hit us head on, is that also the will of Allah?"

I believe that across all religious belief systems there is a belief that the things that happen to us are the will of God. It is very easy to use the terminology of "faith" to conceal fear or even laziness. I believe that God guides us and helps us–I just don't think that he does things for us.

I think about how I parent my own children and when I help them. For example, if I request that one of my boys clean the kitchen, hopefully he would go in and start going to work. If I, as his father, see the big job that he has, I might just roll up my sleeves and give him a hand. Now, what do you think I would do if, as I was scrubbing a pot, my son decided to turn on the television and sit down to catch a show? Well, I can tell what I would do, because I have had to do it in the past. I ask my son why I should help him when he is not doing the work that was his responsibility. Why should I complete his job when he is capable to do it on his own? Simple answer–I won't. Now, I believe that most parents, given the same situation, would have a similar reaction to mine. I would hope so, because reinforcing a child's lack of responsibility and laziness is not good for them.

If we, as parents, or future parents, would interact with our children in this way, doesn't it make sense that God is not going to do things for us that we are capable of doing for ourselves? Faith without action is considered dead. So, if we have faith that God will provide without our action to back that up, we are risking losing that help.

I was speaking with Lily regarding her thoughts of personal responsibility. Lily has the presence of spiritual maturity and has experienced significant loss in her life. Yet not only did she survive through it, she succeeded out of. Lily said, "It gets under my skin when people tell me that God will provide for widows and orphans, then sit back and don't make it happen for themselves." Lily should know, she lived it.

Lily was widowed at thirty-six years old with two children; ages two and eleven. Her husband, Keith survived twenty-two months before he died of a glioblastoma multiform brain tumor at forty-one. She said, "During that time I learned a lot about surrendering to a loving Lord who made promises and kept them. One of those promises was that He would take care of all things concerning us and to absolutely trust Him, which included financial things. I knew God would provide for us, but I didn't know exactly how and most of the time when. I was at home on maternity leave when Keith was diagnosed. In one day, we had no foreseeable financial means. Our insurance did not pay for prescriptions, which averaged six hundred dollars per month, on top of other uncovered expenses. Many wonderful people came forward to help us in many ways, but there were still significant shortages."

Lily continued, "I could not return to my interior design profession because Keith's surgeries and hospitalizations were frequent and I had two small children at home who needed me more than ever. I believed that the Lord would provide for us financially. I watched Christians fall into a belief that they were owed something from the Lord and from other people. They didn't need to do anything – they didn't need to work or go look for work. They expected others to take care of them and if they were not being taken care of like they expected, they blamed people for not obeying God. I didn't believe that, I believed the Lord would provide through many ways and one of those was to lead me to something I could do for myself. And He did.

"For the duration of Keith's illness, I created a hand-painted tableware and tile business. At first, it was very tough because I could not afford the equipment, a kiln, etc... I painted and glazed the pottery in my dining room and at night I carted it down the street to a dear artist friend's house and loaded everything I had into their kiln, which fired through the night until I returned the next morning removed the finished wares and started over again. I worked around Keith's needs and invited friends to my first "open house". Several public shows followed that sold out within the first few hours and much work followed. The work

If we have faith that God will provide without our action to back that up, we are risking losing that help.

was rewarding yet back breaking and financially meager, providing just enough. I constantly reminded myself, that Paul was right when he said, just give me enough – not too much – not too little – then I am content. I was blessed by learning to be content.

"After Keith died, I felt very alone and physically and financially weary. I complained to the Lord that no one was helping me – or not helping me enough. The Lord led me to a life-changing scripture 'The king, moreover, must not acquire great numbers of horses for himself or make the people return to Egypt to get more of them, for the Lord has told you, "You are not to go back that way again."' – Deuteronomy 17:16 Right away, I knew the Lord was telling me – 'Don't go to Egypt for horses because those horses are not what you need – you need to believe that I will deliver you and your children.' Horses were the strength of the army, but the Lord showed in Exodus that He was greater than men and their horses. I didn't need horses. In other words, I didn't need to rely on men or women for help. He promised that He would take care of the widow and the orphans.

"Shortly after, I received a phone call to design a large home–it came at the absolute perfect time. I ended my pottery business and reentered my profession as a residential interior designer. I recently celebrated twenty-six years in the profession with twelve of those years owning my own company. The Lord said He would provide for the widow and the orphans, and He has in a beautiful, loving way."

Personal responsibility leads to action that backs up our faith that God will provide.

Lily recognized that God did not provide her with welfare, he provided her with an opportunity to take care of her. Lily is not the type of person who would become dependent on a hand out. Even in her most trying times, she was willing to stay in the kitchen and work with God's help instead of believing that he would do it for her. This attitude of personal responsibility is largely why Lily has run a thriving and financially lucrative business for several years.

Personal responsibility leads to action and backs up our faith that God will provide. When we provide the action, we allow God to work in our lives. Keep in mind, God does not typically give us the end results of what we want. Instead, he gives us the mechanism to achieve what is in our hearts. If he does all the work for us, that would spoil us and ultimately make us ineffective. I just don't see that happening. So, be prepared to do your share if you are going to take a stand on faith.

Personal responsibility will lead to success

If you are successful in life, you did it! If you are not successful in life, you did it. I know that this statement sounds harsh. But the acceptance of this truth will set you free. Even if you aren't where you would like to be, please understand that you are the architect of your own life. Please understand, you get out of life exactly what you put into it. If a person has the desire to grow, the first place he or she needs to look is in the mirror.

I remember when my son was in swimming lessons. There were several different categories of swimmers, labeled by certain fish. "Junior Lifeguard" was the highest group and what my son was eager to achieve. I recall one of the instructors coming to me and explaining how Dakota was not putting forth the amount of effort to get the skills before qualifying for the Junior Lifeguard class. She was indicating that she could work with him extra and give him a later swim test date. I think I shocked her when I told her, "If he doesn't have it, fail him." Based on her reaction, I don't think she got that from many parents. But my perspective was simple, Dakota wanted to get into the highest class–that is something that is earned, not a right. If he were given an exception to get his goal when he didn't do the necessary work to earn it, it wouldn't be good for him. Yes, he was upset when he didn't get promoted. He cried, and I felt bad for him. I wanted him to feel better, but I wanted him to have a much greater lesson in life–his success is up to him. This was evident the very next set of lessons. When his group moved on and he didn't his motivation to work increased because he wasn't going to miss qualifying for Junior Lifeguard again.

We need to apply the same principle when it comes to our own lives and the lives of other people. When we look outside of ourselves for explanations of our successes or failures, it may feel better, but we ultimately hurt ourselves long term. If I had protected Dakota from his failure, he would have mistakenly believed that he could get results in life without working for them. This perspective would keep him from achieving greater things in his life down the road.

It can be uncomfortable when we get to the point where we shift our focus of blame from something on the outside of us, to focus on ourselves. Nobody likes to be responsible when things aren't going right. The key is, when we focus on things outside, nothing will ever change. We will just keep expecting change and feeling dejected. When we focus on our own effort, it may be harder to accept, but at least we can bring about what we want.

This might be hard to believe, but I would estimate that at least sixty percent of the individuals who schedule an appointment with me are not honestly looking for change. They clearly are not happy with what they feel in life and they honestly want things to be different. But, this group of people tends to look outside of themselves for a way to feel better. Many of them simply look for validation that their lives are miserable, and there is nothing they can do about it.

I look at my role in working with people as providing them with information. I believe that I have compassion for people and the struggles that they face, but I do not wish to enable anybody to fail. If I agree with somebody that there is nothing they can do to make their lives better, they might feel validated, but nothing will change for them. I am honestly willing to sound unfeeling to a person when I am sharing with them that they can take control over their own lives, and they don't have to stay feeling like a victim.

There are many counselors in the field of psychology who, I believe, take on too much personal responsibility for their clients. If their clients do well, the counselor feels successful, like he or she is responsible for that client's success. However, a counselor who is responsible for a client's successes will also have to take responsibility for a different client's failures. I inform clients all the time if they succeed they deserve all the credit. The truth is, if they succeed by applying the information I provide to them, they made their own success happen. How could a person feel successful if I were the one responsible for their progress? It's not possible. It is also not possible that a person could feel successful when they are dependent on someone or something else.

Although it is not enjoyable to look in the mirror, we can only make real and meaningful change in our lives when we become willing to take personal responsibility for our own successes. The good news is that your future is in your hands. The reason this is good news is because nobody is as vested in your success as you are.

The good news is that your future is in your hands.

When we truly wish to help others, we must give them the opportunity to fail. If we insulate their hardships, we rob them of their motivation to succeed.

Take Away Discussion Questions

1. Personal responsibility is one of those universal principles that all people are attracted to. Can you think of an example where someone took responsibility and faced consequences, and earned your respect?

2. Learned helplessness can be a paralyzing feeling. It can seem like no matter what we do, nothing matters–so why try. What do you think is the best way to overcome this state of mind?

3. What do you see as the difference between being victimized and being a victim?

4. How do you imagine someone seeing him or herself as a victim could be a negative controlling influence in their life?

5. Many people try and collect data about their past failures and successes. Why might this attempt work against the pursuit of new goals?

6. Can you think of a situation where someone used God as an excuse to fail in some area of his or her life?

7. I make the statement that "God is not going to do things for us that we are capable of doing for ourselves." Why would such intervention by God not be good for us?

8. Why does scripture say that faith without action is considered dead? How does this principle apply to goal areas in your life?

9. How is it possible that taking 100% of the responsibility for our own situations in life can be an empowering experience?

10. What is the one thing you are going to take away from this chapter and put into practice in your life, starting now?

Chapter 11

You Have to Feel the Burn
The Principle of Pain

> *Character cannot be developed in ease and quiet.*
> *Only through experiences of trial and suffering can the*
> *soul be strengthened, vision cleared, ambition inspired*
> *and success achieved.*

> — *Helen Keller*

A man ventured from his hotel into the backcountry of Mississippi. He parked his car and began walking down a dirt country road. As he observed the old rickety dwellings where people raised their families, he evaluated what he saw as being a simple life. The homes appeared to be only a couple rooms in size. They were built up off the ground and had the raised porch, typically adorned with the classic rocking chair. The yards were simple and often had chickens and goats roaming between wired fences.

This man came upon an old farmer in dirty overalls working in the yard of one of these homes. Some of the farmer's teeth were missing and his face had a leathery texture from years of hard work under the southern sun. The man stopped and struck up a conversation with the farmer about the area, the people, and the culture. The farmer was quite friendly as he leaned on his shovel handle and took a break to talk to the stranger.

As the two men talked, the farmer's hound dog, which appeared to be sleeping in the shade on the porch, let out a big howl. The noise from the dog startled the man, but the farmer didn't even seem to notice. As they continued with their conversation, the hound dog complained even louder a second time. The man looked over as the hound laid his head back on the rickety porch slats. Again, the farmer didn't even acknowledge the dog's whine and just kept on talking about his colorful life in Mississippi. Then, the hound let out an even louder howl. The man thought the dog was trying to communicate to the farmer. He turned to the old man and said, "Sir, what is going on with your dog?" The farmer looked over his shoulder and said with a matter of fact tone, "Oh, he is just laying on a nail sticking up through the boards on the porch." The man, thinking this was crazy, said, "Well why doesn't he move then?" The farmer responded, "It don't hurt that bad."

People respond to adversity much like that hound dog. They have metaphorical spikes in their life that cause them pain. Why don't they do something about it? "It don't hurt that bad."

Pain serves a purpose

"Why is there so much pain in the world?"

"What kind of God could exist if there is so much pain and suffering among his people?"

I have heard these kinds of comments many times, usually from people who have some form of suffering in their life. The answer to these questions might be straightforward, but it doesn't always make people feel better. The answer is that without pain, people couldn't function.

There is a rare medication condition called Congenital Insensitivity to Pain with Anhidrosis or CIPA. When people first think of a life without pain they think it sounds great, but it's not great for people who have the condition. This is a genetic disorder that is present from birth. These children don't sense the heat from a stove or the temperature of food and can easily get burned. They can fall and injure their internal organs, but never know until it's too late. Such children will often have shorter lives due to the complications that can arise due to the absence of pain. Parents with children with this condition say that they would give anything for their child to experience pain.

You see, we have pain for a reason—it lets the body know that something is wrong and needs to be corrected. Experienced pain is like a warning light blinking on the dashboard of your car that draws your attention to a potential problem. Even having a small pebble in your shoe will alert and cause you to stop what you are doing and fix the situation. Larger pains in our bodies will cause us to discontinue activities that could cause greater strain or even damage. Pain notifies us that we need to go to the doctor and get something checked out. Without that pain, we would allow a destructive process to go too far, causing potential irreparable damage.

As I speak about this truth, I realize that there are many people in this world who have chronic pain that they cannot change. I am not trying to minimize what these people go through. Chronic pain can be a very debilitating experience, and some people spend their entire lives going through surgeries, procedures, and treatments trying to find an answer for it. For these individuals, their chronic pain does not serve a purpose.

Pain is a warning system that was designed for our benefit. Like any good system, however, it can go haywire. A security device that an individual installs in her house might get a short circuit and lock her out. A computer on a car to help it run more efficiently could misfire and cause the car to break down. Just because some people have pain that seems to have no explanation, does not take away from the fact that pain was implemented for good reasons.

The idea of accepting the need for pain goes against our cultural beliefs. We live in a pill-popping age. When we want a specific result in our lives, we look for some quick and easy way to get there. We take pills to lose weight, pills to bulk up, pills to feel better, pills to go to sleep, and pills to keep us awake. We want our lives and the lives of others to be pain free, even though that pain serves a purpose for our benefit.

Emotional pain serves the same purpose as physical pain. Pains, such as depression, guilt, shame, and anxiety do not seem to have functional roots to people who experience them. Such issues are treated as if they are some type of cancer that needs to be cut out. Antidepressants are one of the most commonly prescribed classes of medications by family practice physicians. Drugs designed to help us feel better are a multi-billion dollar industry because people who experience emotional pains simply want their suffering to go away.

We want our lives and the lives of others to be pain free, even though that pain serves a purpose for our benefit.

It is much easier to see how physical pain is a warning system for something that might be wrong in our bodies. When we speak of emotional pain as serving a purpose, it can be misinterpreted as victim blaming. People hear, "Your depression is your own fault." This type of statement is not helpful because it only drives someone with an emotional pain deeper into his or her suffering. Someone does not feel emotional pain because they choose to feel it anymore that someone with bronchitis chooses to feel out of breath. But both pains are a symptom of a problem.

Emotional pains are not in our lives to simply torment us–they exist to let us know when there is a problem. When we feel pain, it is an indication that something is wrong and it incentivizes us to change, to grow, and to resolve the problems in our life that causes the pain. Without this pain, we would never develop the motivation to change anything that is not working for us.

One of the most effective treatments for depression is a therapy called Cognitive Behavioral Therapy. The premise of this treatment is helping a person suffering from depression change their thoughts and behaviors to bring about a resulting change in their feelings. This means that the feelings of depression often come from unhealthy thought and action patterns that a person has developed in his or her life. So the cognition and behavior patterns are the pebble in the shoe, which results in the feelings associated with depression. The feelings of depression are then interpreted negatively and acted upon, which leads to more negative feelings. This can create a nasty cycle that spirals a person down, deeper and deeper into a sense of hopelessness and despair. The pain of depressing feelings is supposed to be uncomfortable. That discomfort should create a motivation to get the problems fixed.

Guilt is another warning signal. When we experience a feeling of guilt, it is the light on our dashboard that is warning us that we are doing something that we know to be wrong. For example, if I were to tell somebody a lie as a way to get to the results I wanted, I would probably feel a sense of guilt after the interaction. The reason I would feel guilt is because I believe in the principle of honesty. I desire to be honest with others and I have an expectation that others should be honest with me. So, if I were to violate that principle, guilt would light up in my awareness.

Believe it or not, guilt itself isn't bad. I realize that it has a very negative connotation, usually because it's mislabeled. Guilt is the pebble in the shoe that tells us to stop doing something that is not right and warns us to correct the situation. There is nothing wrong with that. When, however, we choose to feel perpetual guilt or when we transfer guilt to a longstanding sense of shame, this is not healthy. This would be like feeling the pebble in your shoe and doing nothing about it. Can you imagine just constantly grimacing with every step you took with no relief in sight? This is not the warning system that God invented for us. We are not designed to go through life with an ongoing sense of pain. Our purpose is not to live life in a chronic state of guilt or shamefulness.

Feeling pain and doing nothing about it violates the whole
purpose of why we feel pain to begin with.

Most positive, life-changing decisions tend to come out of
adversity. When someone has a good life, they unfortunately
don't experience enough pain to change. We rarely think
that it is unfortunate that someone doesn't have enough
pain. However, people tend to make significant changes in
their lives when they either feel pain or predict the oncoming
of future pain. The seeking of positive
will give us the direction, but it is the
avoidance of pain that will give us the
motive power to accomplish our goals.
People don't change when they see the
light, they wait until they feel the heat.

*People don't
change when
they see the
light, they wait
until they feel
the heat.*

I recall a man in is 50s who had been
carrying excess weight and lacked any
significant physical activity for a long
time. Checkup after checkup doctors told him, "Lose some
weight and start exercising or you are going to have a heart
attack." He listened and took their concerns seriously for
about a week after each appointment. But after a week, the
old patterns started to slip back in and pretty soon the
admonishment from his doctor was a faded memory. That
was until he got out of the shower one morning and
experienced a shooting pain in his shoulder. Without even
having the ability to call to his wife, he collapsed to the floor.
Luckily his wife heard the crash in the bathroom and was able
to dial 911. When he got to the hospital, the doctors
discovered that two of his arteries were 90 percent closed off.
He had to undergo double bypass surgery, which he survived.

You should see this man today. He is fit, active, and looks
20 years younger. He no longer takes his health for granted,
and he listens intently to the advice from his doctors. Even
though he lived the majority of his life developing a negative
health pattern in his life, he was able to completely turn his
life around.

A woman whose husband just left her was feeling an intense level of pain in her life. She said, "But my marriage has already failed, it's too late to do anything about it." She was thinking that since she had already suffered the pain, there was nothing she could do. This is wrong thinking.

People can experience intense negative results throughout their lives. Unless these individuals die from their choices, they can always recover from the negative impact of those consequences. This woman might not have been able to save her marriage, but she can avoid the same thing from happening again. The truth is, most of the time it takes adversity in our lives for us to really make the decision to change.

Balanced pain is productive

Pain has the potential of being overwhelming and all-consuming. Although pain does serve a purpose, too much pain serves as a distraction. I have seen many people who are so focused on the pain in their lives that they do not seem to be able to function. In these cases I absolutely see the benefit of psychotropic medications. If a medication can help a person to stop drowning in their pain so they can focus on changing what they need to change, then medication seems to serve a good purpose. Medication, however, should not be used as a Band-Aid to not feel.

People will make significant changes in their lives for two reasons: For the pursuit of positive goals and for the avoidance of pain. Positive and negative in our lives serve different purposes related to our progress. Goals give direction. Without goals, we tend to wander aimlessly through life. We have to have goals to focus on to know where we want to go. Pain and the avoidance of potential pain give us the motivation to bring about change in our lives. Honestly, pain is a much greater motivator for us to change than wanting something positive in our lives.

Achieving good things in life is a journey that combines the positive things we want and the negative things that we are attempting to avoid. This journey is like a person walking in the middle of a long, dark tunnel. At one end, there is a door that is cracked open enough that the light on the other side can be faintly seen from the person's position. This light represents the positive goals that we set in our lives. The light has the function of removing ourselves from being lost in the darkness of the tunnel. The idea is to journey through the tunnel and move towards our goals and a more positive, successful, position in life.

The other end of the tunnel is completely dark, but there is a sound. The sound is of barking dogs, which is getting louder, indicating that the dogs are approaching. The dogs in this example represent the consequences of negative patterns that will eventually overtake us. These pains could be the result of addiction, emotional problems, relationship problems, financial irresponsibility, passive behavior, laziness, or anything that is non-productive in our lives. We all have the dogs, yet they are different for everybody. They might be called "divorce," "financial hardship," "strained relationships," "job loss," or simply "misery."

We all have negative patterns in our lives. If we don't actively do things to outdistance those patterns, we will suffer the consequences. If those dogs catch up to the person before he reaches the door, they will overtake him and rip him apart. So, the idea is to achieve our positive goals in life before the negative consequences in life overtake us.

People tend to make three basic mistakes in how they divide their attention between their focus on the goals at the end of the tunnel and the dogs approaching out of the darkness. The first mistake is when a person focuses all their attention to the things they want in life. If a person focuses all her attention on her goal to the point of not attending to the dogs, she will mistakenly believe that her goal will be there whenever she needs it. Thus, it is not urgent that she runs after her goal. She can pursue it tomorrow, or next week, or when she feels up to it. With a lack of urgency, this person will walk, rest, get distracted on things along the way, or venture down side tunnels that take her away from her goal. It is similar to the children's story of the tortoise and the hare. The rabbit was so secure in winning the race that he took a nap and ended up losing.

This person might also listen to other people in the tunnel who are failing, but be completely unaware of this fact. People failing might convince this person that the dogs down in the darkness don't really exist, or that she has all the time in the world to reach the goal. They might want her to stop and commiserate with them or join their club. So the woman gets distracted and stops attending to the potential negative coming from the darkness. This woman will have a goal, but lacks the motivation to actively pursue it. This person will be caught unaware when the pack of barking dogs come out of the shadows and maul her.

People also don't feel motivated to run from the dogs because they have the illusion of unlimited time. They know they want something better, and they admit that they are not where they want to be, yet they still don't run toward their goals.

Like the couple that knows they are going in the hole financially, but tell themselves it will turn around somehow. Or how about that couple who know that they are working all the time and not growing in their relationship, but they believe that are still young and have many years to do that. Both couples might hear the barking dogs in the darkness, they know the dogs exist and they have an appropriate level fear. They also see their goals as a way to reach safety. What they do wrong is thinking that they can take their time to accomplish their goals.

Many people believe they can start pursuing their goals tomorrow just as easily as they can today. They wait for the feeling to run after their goals. They don't feel the energy to run today, but maybe they will have a boost of energy tomorrow. But tomorrow never comes. Pretty soon, ten years of tomorrows have passed and the dogs are drawing blood.

The second mistake people make is to spend all their attention focused on the dogs down the tunnel. This is the man who spends all his time focusing on his problems and what kinds of negative things are going to happen to him. He will have high motivation to focus on the approaching dogs. But without direction, he doesn't efficiently pursue his goals to distance himself from the dogs in his life. Even though he sees those dogs as destructive in his life, he will often stand there paralyzed in fear as he stares into the darkness. This man will get so focused on the dogs that he actually allows the dogs to approach. When a person is not facing towards the light at the end of the tunnel, he will trip, take wrong turns, and even act desperately, which causes him to do foolish things. Also, if he focuses on the negative in his life, he will move in that direction. This person may also listen to some people in the tunnel who convince him that the dogs are not his fault, that the world is unfair, and that he needs to sue somebody. Even after this man is attacked and suffers consequences of negative patterns in his life, he might continue to make bad decisions and run into the darkness. This man also rarely makes it through the door and to the achievement of his goals.

Achieving success in anything in life takes a marathon mentality.

Many people are like these persons in the tunnel. They either focus all their energy on a goal, but lack the motivation to pursue it, or they have a great deal of motivation from the focus on the negative, but they lack positive direction to avoid it.

The third mistake that people make is to flip-flop between the first two perspectives. They get mauled by a dog or at least have a legitimate fear generated by the dog then they turn around and sprint toward their goal with 100 percent of their energy. However, they get tired and stop listening to the dogs, so they slow down, focus on other things, and fail to keep moving forward. Then the dogs approach again and they focus all their energy to the negative, which spikes their motivation, yet again and they go from stationary to another sprint. This pattern of movement won't produce what they are looking for.

Achieving success in anything in life takes a marathon mentality. If a person sprints, quits, loses direction, or gets motivated later to enter a different marathon, he or she will never reach the finish line. So, how does a person apply this information to more effectively achieve their goals?

The answer is actually practical. It requires a division of one's attention between the positive goal for direction and the negative consequences for motivation. Much like how we divide our focus between holding the steering wheel for navigation and pressing our foot on the gas petal for power. In the tunnel, however, it is not an equal division. The majority of one's attention needs to be focused forward–let's say 95 percent. The more a person looks back, the more likely he will trip as he attempts to move forward. But he must keep a portion of his awareness on the impending consequences that will be there if no action is taken. The barking dogs should elicit enough fear that the person desires to keep pressing forward to the solution. A person doesn't even have to look over his shoulder to see the dogs, he just has to attend to the seriousness of the threat. He must realize that every time he stops to rest or do non-productive things the dogs get closer. He must recognize that it is a race for him to get through the door before the dogs catch him.

Nobody has all the time in the world. He will not always have the energy to run like he does now. Most people report at the end of their lives that their lives went by faster than they realized. I know this is true for me when I look how fast my own children are growing up.

I recall a man named Tony sitting in my office feeling completely broken. He was crying, not able to function in his job, and had all the classic signs of depression. Tony looked up through his watery eyes and choked out the words, "Why did my wife leave me?" He was asking for the event that happened that moved his marriage from good to bad, "the reason" his wife filed for divorce. It was as if the dog named Divorce suddenly appeared out of nowhere and attacked him when he wasn't looking. Tony could easily convince himself that he was the victim in this scenario–that he was simply doing all the right things and his wife, out of the blue, decided that she didn't want to be married anymore. Tony's feelings are normal, but that is not the way life unfolds.

Tony was the guy in the tunnel who simply was so caught up in what he was doing in his own life that he didn't pay any attention to the fact that divorce was approaching out of the darkness. Tony hung with friends who didn't have good marriages, so when he compared his relationship to theirs, it looked okay. Since he evaluated his marriage based on minimal standards, he didn't realize it was not healthy. His friends told him that he was right in how he talked to and treated his wife. But, anybody with some objectivity in Tony's life could have warned him about the potential destruction of his marriage years before it actually went down. That dog had been barking a long time–Tony simply wasn't listening.

Tony had been self-serving in his marriage. He did what he wanted with little consideration of his wife's needs or desires. He lied to her about where he went in the evenings and barked at her if she asked too many questions. Outward conflict was low around the home because Tony's wife avoided it. When she did raise her concerns and express her needs, Tony suggested that she was being overly emotional or needy. He suggested to her that she had the problems and told her to set an appointment with a psychiatrist to get on some medication. At every turn, Tony choked the life out of his marriage by starving his wife's needs. Through the process, he thought his approach to the marriage was working because his wife complained less and less with time. Without the constant "bitching" from his wife, Tony was able to do more of what he wanted. As she pulled further and

further away from him, Tony was so self-focused that he
didn't see the signs.

Sitting in my office, Tony was feeling ripped apart by the
divorce dog, and there was very little he could do about it. It
had overtaken him with such power that he couldn't stop it.
He suggested to his wife that they go to counseling, but she
was not interested in saving the marriage by that point. She
had reportedly asked him to go to counseling many times
during their seven-year marriage, but he always refused. Now
it was too late. If only he had listened.

Many people like Tony give up the idea of change once a
particular dog, such as divorce, has overtaken them. Because
they tend to see their consequences as something that
happened to them instead of something they brought on
themselves, they don't change. They see the dog that attacked
them as unrelated to their own choices or behavior. So, after
that dog has attacked and moved on, they tend to repeat the
same destructive patterns. This can be very frustrating to
witness.

Many times I have seen people completely destroy their
marriage, only to get remarried within the following year. I
call this, "Different Dog, Same Fleas." This person
externalizes their marriage problems to their ex-spouse or to
some other outside reason, mistakenly believing that another
wife will be easier, or a better fit. The problem is, they take
their fleas (or problems) with them. They bring the same
negative behavior and thought patterns, which contributed to
the downfall of their first marriage, into their second. Guess
what happens? Nothing different. This is one of the reasons
we see an increasing divorce rate related to the more times a
person has been married.

People struggle with finding the balance of living a
positive life and being aware of the impending challenges in
their life. It is important for an individual to take personal
responsibility for both ends of the tunnel. An individual has
the ability to pursue their goals, and they also have the
responsibility for when their choices have caught up to them

and inflicted pain. When we take responsibility and seek balance, we give ourselves a huge boost in our ability to find success in any area of our lives.

Helping too much, hurts others

We not only want to remove the pain in our own lives, we also seek to remove the pain from other people. When we see pain as bad or evil, we feel an obligation to keep others from experiencing it. Nobody in their right mind wishes suffering on others. We all have a sense of connection to other people and that compassion allows us to feel bad when others are in pain. This compassion creates a natural desire in the hearts of many people to help others. All in all this is good. We need to be focused on other people and show acts of compassion and love.

There is, however, a very fine line between serving the needs of others and enabling them. When we focus on keeping others from pain in their lives, there is a strong likelihood that we are not serving their best interests. If we understand that pain serves a purpose, then when we remove the pain, we remove the mechanism for change.

Simply put, when a person's life is pain and consequence free, they have no reason to change. From the former example of the dogs in the tunnel, if we could somehow remove the dogs from life, the person in the tunnel would likely never feel the urgency to pursue their goals. The darkness of the tunnel would be a satisfactory life.

Laura was admiring her rose bushes the other day. They are quite impressive, even for a guy who doesn't know much about flowers. The bushes were about seven feet tall and just filled with buds that were beginning to bloom in a variety of vibrant colors. As we were standing there, Laura said that the reason the bushes are blooming with such abundance is because she significantly pruned them back earlier in the season. She explained that pruning process allowed the rose bushes to come back even greater than they were before. It dawned on me that these rose bushes are just like people. When we get pruned through adversity and painful experiences in life, we have the opportunity to come back stronger, brighter, and closer to our potential.

But just like those rose bushes, when we don't face adversity, we don't tend to change. When we don't change, we don't grow. When we aren't growing, we are actually dying. As a result of that process in dealing with others, when we remove the pain from their lives, we affect their motivation to grow. In the short run we may be making someone's life easier, but in the long run, we are harming him or her. Most of the time people leap across this line of helping others with the greatest intentions in the world, only to cause more problems than they can fix.

Kelli was a thirty-year-old woman who was married and had three children. She was one of those women who were constantly volunteering her time running Sunday school classes for her church and helping anybody who had a need. She was so much of a giver that she developed a reputation of the person who would do it when nobody else would. Kelli believed that she needed to give of herself because that was what God wanted her to do. She also desperately wanted to please others. As a result, Kelli felt drained much of the time and believed that others took her for granted.

> *Most of the time people leap across this line of helping others with the greatest intentions in the world, only to cause more problems than they can fix.*

I recall talking to Kelli one time when she mentioned that she needed to take her brother and his wife to the airport. Kelli explained that her brother asked her to drive them to the airport so they didn't have to pay for parking during their trip. She said that she was driving about 30 miles to pick up her brother and his wife, and then driving them back to the airport, which was in the general area of where she lived. I asked Kelli why she was going so far out of her way to drive her family when they were capable of driving themselves? Kelli stated that her brother and his wife were not Christians and she wanted to demonstrate to them how Christians are good people. I explained to Kelli, that she was not helping her brother–that he was actually taking advantage of her. The only thing he was learning about her or Christians is that they can be manipulated.

Come to find out, Kelli described her brother as self-centered and superficial in relationships. Thus, since he asked Kelli to take her time and money to drive them so they could save money, it was a selfish act. When Kelli agreed, she rewarded his negative relationship pattern.

You see, when we do things for people that they are capable of doing themselves, but choose not to, we hurt them. We're not serving people by giving them what they need–we are enabling them by giving them what they want. People usually don't want the things they need and don't need the things that they want. This dynamic makes serving other people a hard job.

I spoke with Kelli a few months after this incident and asked her what she did. She told me that she set a boundary with her brother that if he wanted her to take them to the airport they could drive to her house. She said that it felt good and she did not feel like they were taking advantage of her. Even better, her brother has decreased his demands on her.

Rob and Linda were parents in their fifties. They had two young adult sons and a teenage daughter. Rob and Linda loved all their children, but their boys had really made a mess of their lives. They were both in their early twenties and just were not making responsible decisions. They would lose their jobs and sit in their apartment for several weeks playing video games instead of looking for work. When it came time for their rent, they clearly didn't have the money to stay, so they went to mom and dad. Now, both Rob and Linda were intelligent people. They knew that their boys were being irresponsible, but they just couldn't stand the idea of them not having a place to live. They imagined that if their sons were kicked out they would be homeless, which could lead to increased drug use and even death. So, Rob and Linda stepped in again and again, trying to "help" their boys.

Unfortunately, each and every time Rob and Linda came to their boys' rescue, they were expounding the problem. See, the boys learned that they didn't have to be responsible and that somebody would make it okay. The boys never experienced the hard consequences for the poor decisions they made, so they kept making bigger poor decisions. As the problems went on, the stakes got higher. By the time Rob and Linda were fed up with their boys' righteous attitudes and self-serving irresponsible decisions, the pattern was well established. I recall Linda getting so frustrated with the escalation of destruction of her boys that she yelled at them that she wanted them out of her life.

Linda's response was a typical outcome for when we have spent considerable time enabling others. When we violate good boundaries and give too much to others, we tend to foster dependency and taking-focused behaviors. We give because we believe that if this other person just had a break they could get on their feet. The problem is we don't give them a reason to get off the floor. When we continue to give, but nothing is reciprocated, we become resentful for our continued vulnerability. When this happens, we tend to swing to the opposite side of the continuum and we draw a hard line. The line is like a wall that we build out of bricks to protect us from being taken advantage of again. It is self-protective, and honestly, still not a good balance of interaction with others.

I reminded Rob and Linda of good parental boundaries in the story of the prodigal son. In the book of Luke, Jesus tells a parable of a father whose son goes astray. The younger of two sons asked for his portion of his inheritance. When his father gave him his share, he took the money and ran, squandering his resources on the pleasures of life. He blew everything he had and eventually found himself seeking a needed meal in a pigs' trough. The boy had fallen as low as he could go when he realized that his father's servants had food to spare, yet he was starving. This boy hit bottom and made a decision to humble himself to his father. He readied himself to return to his father, beg forgiveness, and assume the role of a servant. His righteousness was gone. When the father saw the boy coming across the field, he ran to the boy and celebrated his return. He didn't make his son become a servant. He embraced his son and rejoiced that he had come home. The father held the perspective that his son had died, but was alive again.

The important lesson in this parable is how the father dealt with his son. He didn't go chasing after him and trying to convince him that blowing all his money was bad. He didn't find him in the pig trough and take him out to dinner so he didn't have to eat slop. This father allowed his son the opportunity to hit bottom while he maintained the stability of his own farm and family. The son had to save himself. When this son decided to change and developed a repenting heart, his father didn't hold grudges. The story doesn't say anything about the father sitting the son down and giving him a three-hour lecture on fiscal responsibility. This father allowed life to be the teacher.

Enabling somebody also harms our relationship with him or her. When we give an individual too much of what they want or believe they deserve, they begin to become dependent on the gift. The receiver in this situation will tend to take and take some more, constantly pushing the limits of the giver to the point where the giver starts feeling resentful or taken advantage of. Once the individual who is giving starts to realize that the support given is not helping the other person to change and make their own life better, their willingness to give is turned off. Once this happens, the

Loving someone sometimes means allowing him or her to fail.

person who has been receiving the subsistence develops a righteous indignation towards the giver's callousness or insensitivity. After this ongoing relationship of support and generosity, the giver is only seen in a negative light once a proper serving boundary is put into place. I have personally witnessed many, many relationships destroyed because of this initial good intention.

We need to understand that pain serves a purpose, not only for ourselves, but for others as well. Truly loving someone and showing honest compassion is not always popular because it sometimes involves setting boundaries and not giving people what they think they deserve. Loving someone sometimes means allowing them to fail—because only through their failure will they have the opportunity to bloom brighter during the rest of their life.

Take Away Discussion Questions

1. Remember that hound dog, who simply complains about the pain but doesn't do anything about it? We all have spikes in our lives. What are some of yours that you haven't moved off of?

2. God gave us the ability to feel pain because we are designed to fix things that are wrong in our lives. How has this played out for you?

3. How might a pain-free life turn into a stagnant life?

4. What might happen to individuals who attempt to use a shortcut to remove pain in their life?

5. In the analogy of the person in the tunnel with the barking dogs, people make three basic mistakes in their focus. Which one, or ones of these errors do you evaluate yourself doing?

6. What do you think would change in your life if you kept the majority of your focus on the positive goals and maintained an awareness of the potential pain?

7. Most negative things that happen to us are not coincidence or bad luck, they are the natural consequences of the patterns of choices we have made in life. How does this realization help us move forward?

8. Once you understand how pain serves a purpose in your own life, extend that concept to your dealings with others. What might this look like?

9. Loving somebody is not easy work. Truly loving people is learning how to set appropriate boundaries with them so that we give them the greatest opportunity for growth in their own lives. How could you put this concept into practice?

10. What is the one thing you are going to take away from this chapter and put into practice in your life, starting now?

Chapter 12

Feeling Good For Good Reasons
The Principle of Value

> *We gain strength, and courage, and confidence by*
> *each experience in which we really stop to look fear in*
> *the face ... we must do that which we think we cannot.*

— *Eleanor Roosevelt*

Thomas likely became a farmer due to illiteracy and a lack of education. He could barely write his name and never set positive goals in his life. Thomas lived a selfish life, which made him a poor excuse for a father. After his first wife died, he abandoned his nine-year-old son and eleven-year-old daughter to fend for themselves for six months in an isolated cabin deep in the woods. This young boy was left to deal with his mother's death and even had to whittle wooden pegs for her coffin.

During their time alone, the children nearly starved to death. When Thomas returned after being away for so many months, he introduced his kids to their new mother who he'd met on his journey. Thomas did nothing to promote a relationship with his son. He gave him an axe at the age of seven and put him to work clearing their property. He never encouraged education or achievement of any kind. In fact, when his son picked up a book, Thomas made fun of him.

As this son grew up, he did not get along well with his father. His father was not a man of character and never sowed positive to build the esteem of this boy. Yet, this young man developed his own character and confidence. He began supporting himself at a young age by working long hours in menial jobs and eventually became educated against the odds of his upbringing. After two separate failed business attempts and losing money he didn't have, he went back to school to become a lawyer.

As a lawyer, this man's reputation for honesty and integrity started to come to light. For example, he didn't like to charge people who were as poor as he'd been. Once a man sent him twenty-five dollars, but this lawyer sent ten dollars back, saying the man was being too generous. He often convinced his clients to settle their issue out of court, saving them a lot of money, and earning nothing for himself. There is a story about the old widow of a soldier, who was being charged two hundred dollars for getting her four hundred dollar pension. This lawyer sued the pension agent and won the case for the old woman. He didn't charge her for his services—in fact, he paid her hotel bill and gave her money to buy a ticket home.

By most standards this man would be considered a fool. He gave away money he didn't have. He told the truth and did the right things, even when it cost him financially.

This man had many setbacks in his life. At one point he asked a beautiful woman to marry him, but during their engagement she suddenly died. He made several attempts to enter politics, yet just couldn't seem to get elected. Through failure after failure in his life, he continued to approach life with character-based decisions. As he kept doing the right things, he built his sense of solid self-esteem.

Eventually, his persistence and established confidence paid off. In 1860 he was elected President of the United States. Even with all his failures, Abraham Lincoln is described as being one of the most confident men to ever enter the presidency. Abraham Lincoln is one of my favorite individuals from history because he did it right. Lincoln persisted with the philosophy of living his life based on principles. Although he didn't experience immediate successes in his life, his honesty and character are still talked about to this day.

Lincoln's philosophy of confidence and self-identity can be discovered in his own statements:

> *Honesty makes you feel good about yourself and creates trust in others. It improves your relationship with yourself and with others. It's not much in fashion these days to talk about the benefits of honesty and decency, but the benefits are there and they are valuable and worth the trouble.*
>
> *Every man is proud of what he does well; and no man is proud of what he does not do well. With the former, his heart is in his work; and he will do twice as much of it with less fatigue. The latter performs a little imperfectly, looks at it in disgust, turns from it, and imagines himself exceedingly tired. The little he has done, comes to nothing, for want of finishing.*
>
> *Adhere to your purpose and you will soon feel as well as you ever did. On the contrary, if you falter, and give up, you will lose the power of keeping any resolution, and will regret it all your life.*

Have you ever wondered how some people seem to feel really good about themselves? Abraham Lincoln gave us the answer to self-esteem. The pathway to increased self-esteem is found in making consistent principle-based decisions in one's life.

Everybody battles with confidence

Confidence and self-esteem are related. We tend to think about self-esteem as our inner evaluation of our abilities and worth. Confidence is the external manifestation of that value. When we have positive self-esteem, we will show good confidence. If we have low self-esteem, our behavior will reveal that insecurity in some way.

It sure seems like some people just don't have problems with self-esteem and confidence. It's like they were born happy and have simply gone through life with that same level of excitement and enthusiasm. There are, of course, people who have positive outlooks on life and those who have negative outlooks. There are people who feel better about themselves, and those who feel worse. But it is important to realize that nobody on the planet has perfect self-esteem. We all have areas of insecurity in our lives. This is an inherent issue, with which every single person in the human race struggles.

There are two basic errors that people make when it comes to evaluating self-esteem. First of all, they believe that they are alone in their struggle with low self-esteem. They know how they feel inside, and then they evaluate their interpretation of how others experience life. They know their own fears, and they wrongly evaluate that other people don't struggle with issues like them. They basically compare their hidden stuff with the displayed presentation of other people. Friends, when people do this, they will always fall short. What you see on the outside of someone else is not always an accurate presentation of what is actually under the surface.

Many people look good and smell good, but they are stinking on the inside.

What is the pat answer to the question "How are you doing?" "Fine." The truth is, however, their lives aren't fine. Many people look good and smell good, but they are stinking on the inside. It is important to realize that a person is not alone when they battle with confidence or self-esteem.

The second major error I see people make is when they believe that they are above self-esteem or confidence issues. I have had business leaders who have questioned my statement that everybody has insecurity. They have argued that they don't have insecurity, and their confidence is solid. Of course, these are the same guys who cannot stand to be wrong and show high levels of defensiveness to other people, oftentimes including their wives.

Honestly, some of the people who are most outspoken about their confidence are just wearing a mask. Margaret Thatcher once said, "Being powerful is like being a lady. If you have to tell people you are, you aren't." Having confidence is the same thing. Many people go around trying to show or prove their confidence and positive self-esteem. They may act in control, but if they have to demonstrate it, it is not true confidence.

There is a huge difference between confidence and arrogance. Arrogance is a showing off of confidence behaviors that are intended to promote greatness of self. Someone who is arrogant tries to assert that they are better than others. They have weaknesses in their life, but they don't want to admit them for fear of losing their sense of superiority. Arrogant people lack humility. Their arrogance is a mask that they wear to feed their own egos. They might act confidently, but they are not being honest with themselves about who they are to their core.

Ego stands for "Erasing God Out." When a person gets to a point in their life where they think they are great, they believe they don't need anything from anybody, including God. This is unfortunate because Jesus told us that if you want to be first, you must put yourself last. To reach our potential, we must achieve a healthy humility. When we can comprehend that we are no worse and no better than anybody else, we

Ego stands for "Erasing God Out."

make great progress to our own sense of self. The corollary to Jesus' statement is that if you put yourself first, you will end up being last. When we erroneously believe that we are smart enough, strong enough, and gifted enough that we don't need anything, we are overfeeding our ego and we limit our ability to succeed.

In true confidence, a person acts sure of himself or herself all the way down to his or her core. The way they present themselves is sincere. At their core, they recognize that they are no better or worse than anybody else, so their confidence is based in humility. They understand they have weaknesses and, therefore, they don't try to hide them. Such confident people get their sense of ability, not on them being great, but believing in something greater than themselves. They feel capable in life because they have demonstrated their ability to succeed.

Some people don't act arrogantly across the board, they just don't venture out of their comfort zone. Thus, they appear to be confident, because they only play the games in life they know they can win. Because of this, people who have high levels of success in one or two areas are sometimes the most difficult people to work with. They might not have success somewhere in their life, but they often refuse to look at it because that is uncomfortable. So, they continually revert back to areas in their life where they already feel successful and they camp out there.

Charlie and Kathy are a couple who both struggled with humility in their relationship. Charlie was a quiet guy, but a completely gifted businessman who didn't even blink when he made a million dollars. Kathy was a strong woman who felt in her element when she was directing and controlling something or someone. Charlie and Kathy came in for marriage counseling after about sixteen years of a difficult marriage with very poor communication. They were both highly intelligent and competent individuals who refused to stay in the vulnerability and humility of counseling for their marriage problems. Charlie would often not show up for counseling sessions because he had a scheduling conflict and had to attend to his investors. He would rather stay in an arena were he felt successful than come to a counseling session where he felt like he was losing in his own family. Kathy was frustrated with Charlie's lack of priority for marital counseling. She was willing to give up all the money to have a healthy marriage, but she wasn't willing to give up her control. Even when we discussed how her cutting words to her husband drove him away from her, she continued to revert back to those very words in the moment because she felt in control when she spoke her mind. They both hated the feeling of vulnerability and thus didn't keep doing the right things in their marriage. The problem is, old patterns brought about the same old consequences.

I understand what it feels like to want to stay in areas where the success has been established. It is so easy to simply hide out where it feels safe. For example, I feel quite competent to work with individuals in a one-on-one setting. I have given counsel to individuals who have much more financial success than me. I have provided counseling to individuals who have more advanced degrees and, in my opinion, have me beat hands down in the intelligence factor. I have even shared biblical principles with Bible scholars, who I know have a much more in-depth understanding of scripture than me. It is interesting, but in my one-on-one setting in my office I usually feel pretty good about my abilities.

Yet, take me out of that setting and we move to uncharted territory. I have questioned my ability to accomplish many things in my life. As soon as the game changes, I realize that my confidence tends to drop. Even the goal of writing this book and getting it published was quite a shocker for me. I just assumed that all the stuff I talk about every day would naturally flow into the pages and the birds would sing to me as my fingers tried to keep up with my thoughts. That lasted about 10 minutes. There were a couple of incidents early in the process that shook my confidence. The first one really hit me early in the writing phase of this book when I walked into a Barnes and Noble and stood there looking at all the books. There are hundreds of authors out there who have written on living successfully. These men and women seem to have very insightful ways to communicate their points. Some of them pump out another book a couple times a year. I had thoughts like "Why would anybody buy a book written by me when there are shelves upon shelves of other books?" I remember telling Laura, "I don't want to go into Barnes and Noble again until I am done."

Another incident occurred after I was into the project for a few months. I picked up an earlier chapter and read it. When I was done, I realized that I couldn't even follow my own logic. After calling it quits early that night with a copy of that chapter thrown on the floor, I decided to reorganize and reformat much of what I had written. It was hard on me. Both of those situations stand out in my mind of me questioning my ability and the likelihood of success.

Doubt in our abilities just comes with the territory. When we are honest with ourselves, we realize that we all have flaws and weaknesses. We all question our abilities, our spiritual connectedness, our relationships, and our inherent value. I think about the disciples who learned directly from Jesus, yet they still had doubt in what they were doing. My thinking is, if the apostle Peter had doubt even after he walked on water, I think it is an issue that we all face.

Value is found on the inside

The path to self-esteem is not that difficult to find. For most of us, the path is right before our eyes, but it's disguised. Thomas Edison once said, "Opportunity is missed by most people because it is dressed in overalls and looks like work." Confidence and self-esteem follows the same concept. The truth is, individuals will never find self-esteem in something outside of themselves. People need to stop looking for quick fixes. They will not be happy if they have a date, or husband, or new job, or even a million bucks.

"I don't know, I would like to try and see if a million dollars would make me feel better," a woman once told me.

There is no question that a million dollars would probably relieve some of the stress in our lives. We could get out of debt, travel more, and do the things that would bring more enjoyment into our lives. But, there are a lot of wealthy, yet miserable people out there. Money is nice, but you cannot buy self-esteem. Self-esteem does not come from money or things. One can only feel better about oneself once they understand principles and start living their lives by them.

Most people look for things outside themselves as a way to feel better. They believe that if they get better clothes, more money, different friends, a different job, a different spouse, or even a different nose, they would feel better about themselves. These things give us the impression that they work to improve self-esteem because we get a short-term boost. The day that you drive that red convertible sports car off the lot, you tend to sit a little straighter and you feel like you are on top of the world. You go out and wash the car in your driveway so all the neighbors can see. But how long does that feeling last? Maybe a couple of months. Then that car is just a car again. The boost in self-esteem is gone and you are back where you started. The shot of positive self-esteem people get from each of these endeavors keeps many people looking to the outside for more. That is why they don't tend to find it.

Your value does not come from your performance.

Many people also look to performance-based value in their lives. Much of the time this comes from early programming from parents and schools. Children are given value for being pretty, athletic, skinny, funny, and producing results such as grades and awards. Likewise, some children are criticized for being homely, clumsy, fat, boring, and average. When individuals who experienced this type of reinforcement in childhood grow up, they continue to see their value in these superficial realms.

It's not just the individuals who got the negative comments who have low self-esteem. I have seen many strikingly beautiful women who cannot see any value in who they are as a person. When individuals start finding their value or lack of value in the superficial, performance based arena, they continue down that same path much of their lives. They seek words of approval from others and look to promotion and accomplishment to find their self-worth. The problem is, no matter how much weight they lose, how many times they visit the plastic surgeon, how far they climb that ladder in the corporate world, or how many softball trophies they win, it will never be enough. Your value does not come from your performance. Looking to performance for our worth is still looking on the outside of us.

Sometimes the things we pursue leave a deeper hole in our self-esteem than when we started. Addictions that people suffer from are a good example of this. I have had quite a bit of experience in working with men who have sexual addictions. These guys will regularly gravitate to pornography, strip clubs, promiscuous sexual encounters, and even prostitution. Every single time they are tempted to engage in their addictive pattern, it comes from a feeling of emptiness in themselves, a missing confidence and esteem. This hole in their emotion needs to be filled and the sexual addiction does it quite well–temporarily. The let down, however, is fairly dramatic. Typically, it doesn't take but a few minutes after the addictive cycle before the regret and guilt come to the surface and creates a bigger hole. Thus, even though they try to fill it with something on the outside, their sexually impulsive behavior only makes their self-image worse.

Some people look to philosophy, religion, or science to try and understand who they are. Again, they are looking in the wrong places and never feel like they make progress in their own lives. The reason is self-esteem does not come in the form of education or insight. If insight was all that was needed, one could simply read the Bible and hear the verses that God is no respecter of persons or that he values you so much that the hairs on your head are numbered and instantly feel worthwhile and valued. Although these scriptures and that conclusion are true, it just doesn't seem to help people feel better about themselves. They read those scriptures and think that God is talking about everybody except them–that somehow those statements don't seem to fit with their emotional evaluation of themselves.

There have been many people who have told me, "Yes Todd, I understand that God loves all people and sees me no better or worse than any other person, but I don't feel it's true for me." Again, these people are looking for their self-esteem in something outside of themselves. Keep in mind God will not shove a positive self-image down anybody's throat. God is an answer, but not through insight or study, but through faith. And remember God tells us that faith without action is considered dead. So if we are going to look to God to find our value, we have a responsibility on our end of that deal. This requires us to act consistently with how God sees us–only then will we reap the positive feelings of our true value.

People mistakenly try to change their feelings about themselves directly. This will never work. We cannot decide to feel good about ourselves and then wake up the next day with a new vitality for life. We don't just decide to feel better and the happiness flows in. It doesn't work to change feelings directly–we only can bring about a change in how we feel through a change in our thoughts and behaviors. To feel better about ourselves, we must understand that we have to do the things that confident and stable people do. Our success in growing our self-esteem is also dressed in overalls and disguised as work.

Confidence comes from banking good decisions

It can sure seem like confidence is unfairly distributed across all people. The truth is, confidence *is* unfairly distributed. Confidence is like a bank account. Some people have huge accounts and some people are overdrawn. This inequality between people is not based in some sort of fate or uncontrollable forces. In most regards people have an active role in how much is in their accounts.

The same principles apply to both confidence and money. If you bank positive into your account, you build a positive balance. If you withdraw and detract from your account, you deplete your resources.

The development of confidence is easy to see in the learning of a skill. For example, when a teenager is just learning to drive, he is unsure of everything he does. He fails to react or overreacts to situations because he lacks confidence in his abilities. As he drives and gains more experience, his confidence is affected. If he makes good decisions about his driving, he builds confidence. The more times he faces challenging situations and overcomes, the more he begins to believe he is a competent driver. If, however, he doesn't pay attention and gets into several wrecks, he will grow his insecurity. What he does behind the wheel will add or subtract from his driving confidence account.

Confidence related to strong self-esteem is developed through the same process. Just like how we can make good decisions behind the wheel of a car, we can make good decisions based on principles. When we make right decisions about life, we bank self-esteem and real confidence.

Most people know the things they should be doing in their life. They know they shouldn't be lazy and watch television for tyenty-four hours per week. They realize they shouldn't be impulsive and blow their money on useless items. They understand that they should tell the truth and take the high road. They believe in the Golden Rule and that they shouldn't act in such a way that hurts others. People have a conscience that gives them the ability to know right from wrong. This moral guide seems to be present in most people regardless of religious beliefs.

In some extreme cases a person's conscience has been reprogrammed by evil influences. It is unfortunate when individuals are raised in environments that promote hate, intolerance, or criminal acceptance. When people are raised with negative as the norm in their life, they often don't comprehend the difference between right and wrong anymore.

For the majority of us, however, we know when we are doing the right things. In fact, if we end up doing the wrong things we have to justify it to make ourselves feel okay about it. People engage in this type of rationalization process regularly. It is interesting to observe the creative process when people realign the facts in their minds to come to the conclusion that matches their feelings or behaviors. This occurs frequently when people justify a divorce as being in the "best interests of the kids." Although there are some cases where this is true, they are more of the exception.

When a person goes through life trying to convince himself that there is no ultimate right or wrong, he is the one who ends up suffering. I remember meeting with a young man who identified himself as Agnostic. An Agnostic is a person who doesn't commit to a belief about God. Unlike an Atheist, who actually has a religion of "no God," an Agnostic person tends to be searching and questioning. This young man was one of the most depressed persons I had ever seen. He had no goals, no direction, and approached life with the same apathy as he did with his spirituality. He didn't believe in anything. He had no acknowledgment of right or wrong,

When we fail to accept the truth we are voluntarily placing ourselves in a form of bondage.

good or evil, even moral or immoral. The result of his perspective was his feeling of drifting aimlessly through life. Although he attempted to convince himself that there were no ultimate truths, this only created a sense of hopelessness for his own mind. He reasoned himself right out of his life having meaning. This created a separation from his mind and sprit.

Many people believe that the acceptance of right and wrong is limiting. The truth is, when we accept that there is right and wrong, we are simply acknowledging what our conscience already knows. Jesus stated that the truth will set us free. When we fail to accept the truth we are voluntarily placing ourselves in a form of bondage. We can try to use our intellect to override truth, but we will never feel good about ourselves when our own conscience knows that we are living a lie.

When we don't acknowledge good principles and how they apply to life, there is no framework for our decisions and actions. Thus, we tend to be inconsistent and ineffective in how we handle life. The more we evaluate our ineffectiveness, the more we label ourselves to have low self-esteem. This is a downward spiraling cycle into a pit of despair.

Confidence is an evaluation judgment based on the decisions we make through life. If we quit everything we start, we tend to see ourselves as a quitter. If we give in to our fear on a regular basis, we see ourselves as weak or afraid. Our thoughts lock in the impressions we get of our confidence and self-esteem.

For example, there is a guy who sees himself as shy. Because he lacks confidence around women, he has anxiety and fear to talk to them. He has read books on communicating and how to date with style. So, he stands in line behind a woman at the coffee shop and thinks about all the right things to say. But his fear keeps him from opening his mouth and the opportunity passes. How does this guy evaluate himself after this situation? He probably says something to himself like, "You wimp, what is wrong with you? You had your chance, and you blew it. You will never be successful with women!"

His self-imposed tirade chips away at his already low self-esteem. Every time he goes through this type of process, his evaluation of himself worsens. This guy could read every book on dating that exists and it wouldn't help his confidence. The only thing that would get him out of this slump is to prove to himself that he can overcome. He has to do the things that he is afraid of doing so he can change his negative self-evaluation.

When we accept that there are established principles that will lead us to live a successful life, we can discipline ourselves to do the right things. This is how we bank solid self-esteem. Just like the negative pattern can be a vicious cycle, a positive pattern can be a victorious cycle.

When we know that we are making the right choices and not giving into things like fear, doubt, shame, impulse, or insecurity, we begin to feel better about ourselves. Then, when we begin to see the results unfold in our lives from the good choices we make. Good choices lead to good results–this process is like making regular deposits into our self-esteem bank account.

Many people don't understand the principles of banking anything. They mistakenly believe that they have to bank large sums in order to achieve a goal of a growing account. Therefore, they don't tend to discipline themselves on a daily basis, thinking the small decisions are unimportant. The truth is, it is the little good choices that people make on a regular basis that will produce greatest positive results. It is not waiting until you have an extra ten thousand dollars to put into your account–it is dropping that fifty or one hundred dollars out of every paycheck into your savings instead of blowing it on fast food. Financial planners tell us that the non-discretionary spending that we engage in on a daily basis is what sinks us financially.

To build self-esteem, the process is found in the small things.

It is the daily habit of four dollars every morning for coffee, five dollars every afternoon for the combo-meal, and the dollar fifty for a soda and chips. That weekly habit is over two hundred dollars per month.

Just like with money, banking self-esteem requires the same daily attention to the small details of life. Many people tend to look for the big things they can achieve to give their confidence a boost. They even look to things outside of themselves, like cars, clothes, money, or good looking dates to give their account a large deposit. This is why so many people simply don't build their self-esteem. To build self-esteem, the process is found in the small things. It is paying attention to the daily disciplines of doing the right things every day, not a big score. We have to watch the decisions we make on a daily basis because they are much more powerful than we give them credit.

Every decision we make goes into our self-evaluation. We can attempt to lie to ourselves, but we can't lie to our conscience. Because we know good from bad, we must choose as many good decisions as we can. This is how we begin to bank a positive self-image.

Take Away Discussion Questions

1. People make one of two errors when it comes to evaluating their confidence: they either believe that they have lower self-esteem than most other people and are destined to have no value, or they believe they don't have insecurity and esteem issues in their life. Which one of these patterns do you see yourself falling into?

2. How do you think it is possible that facing something negative in your life can have the resulting feeling of freedom?

3. In what ways have you found yourself looking towards external things or factors in your life as a way to feel better about yourself?

4. People cannot simply tell themselves something positive and feel better about them. They must put their positive thoughts into action. What is something you can do to push yourself out of your comfort zone and build confidence?

5. If you try to please everybody you will feel like a fake, and this will destroy your confidence in your own self-evaluation. Are there areas in your life where you don't stand up for what you believe to be true?

6. Embrace today. Your self-evaluation will not be determined by grand gestures–it will come from the daily building blocks you put into your life. What is something, even small, that you can do today that will put you on a good path?

7. How might your life be better when you overcome fears, doubt in yourself, and insecurity?

8. What would it look like to start behaving consistently with how God views you?

9. What are three principles you learned from this book that you are going to put into practice and discipline yourself to address on a daily basis?

10. What is the one thing you are going to take away from this chapter and put into practice in your life, starting now?

Principle-based decisions brings it all together

There is a result for every decision that we make–rewards for good decisions and consequences for poor decisions. Many people minimize the impact of their choices on a day-to-day basis because they don't see the direct connection to corresponding results in their lives. They end up making poor choice after poor choice, then wondering why things never seem to work out the way they want.

Every decision has an impact on our future, much like how throwing a rock into a pond creates a ripple effect that extends way beyond the point of impact. One rock in the middle of the pond can create a wave that will reach the shore. One choice in a person's life can also have a ripple effect that will carry into their future and even extend into their children and grandchildren's lifetimes.

There is no such thing as an isolated, unrelated, or meaningless decision. Well, possibly your choice between Coke and Pepsi is insignificant, unless you happen to own one of those companies. But even small decisions, such as what books you choose to read or the people you surround yourself with, can be significantly influential to the direction you life takes.

In order to reach our fullest potential, we must take captive the decisions we make on a daily basis. Otherwise our thoughts run wild, which leads to a lack of purposefulness and results in drifting through life. Goals are hard (if not impossible) to hit if we don't aim at them.

Making productive and positive decisions takes constant attention, much like keeping a plane airborne. Staying in the air is never the default for a plane–the pilot has to keep focused to ensure that the plane doesn't lose altitude and crash to the ground. Positive, productive, principle-based, character-building decisions are rarely the easy ones. Our selfishness, fears, doubt, and laziness are like gravity in how they contribute to the ease of negative and non-productive decisions, which pulls us to where we don't want to be–crashing and burning.

One of the best decisions you can make is to remind yourself everyday that you have a potential that is much greater than you can imagine. God created you with power and abilities beyond your awareness, and maybe even your comprehension. You are a creation out of perfection, not dysfunction. People of influence, including you, have used your past experiences to falsely label you and limit your capabilities. God does not see these limitations; therefore, they are not factored into his evaluation of your potential.

Stop drawing conclusions about your future based on your past. You are not a mindless machine that simply runs predetermined programs. Unhealthy parents, hardships, traumas, abuse, being the wrong sex/race, or living through an economic disaster does not define who you are nor who you can become. Your future is not dictated by what you got wrong during your lifetime. In fact, it is the adversities you have faced in your life that will shape the strength and depth of your character and lead you to be even more impactful to others. Your hardships and failures can be seen as a curse or a blessing–you get to choose their influence on your future.

God is not going to force you to become anything. Don't confuse your potential with your fate. Even though your potential is huge, your free will is going to override any process of growth. If God placed inside of you the ability to impact millions of people in a positive way, yet you choose to sit on your couch in the evenings laughing at mind-numbing sitcoms and spend your days complaining about how hard your life is, your lack of self-discipline, not your potential, is the determining factor for your destiny. God loves you so much that he will not interfere with your life, and thus allow you to fail miserably if that is your will.

It is vital to see yourself from God's perspective and just as essential to think and act according to that potential in your life. The book of James states, "In the same way, faith by itself, if it is not accompanied by action, is dead" (James 2:17 NIV). It's too easy to say we have faith that God wants good things for us. It is a different deal all together to act according to that faith with our daily decisions, especially since much of the time there is a lack of evidence when it comes to our potential. Step out on faith. Don't use doubt, fear, or "evidence" to make your decisions. Faith means that you act according to how God sees your future, not how you see your past.

Once you recognize the potential within you, as seen through God's eyes, you have a responsibility to get up, get moving, and make things happen in your own life. Henry Ford said, "Whether you believe you can do a thing or not, you are right." You, and all other people, will fail to grow in any area of life when there is a failure to embrace greater possibilities. The destiny in front of you is an unwritten chapter in a book with an end that hasn't yet been determined. How your story ends is completely based on the choices you start making today.

Fortunately, you don't have to guess what those positive choices are. God gives you the blueprint for success, and all you have to do is believe in his desires for your life and discipline your thoughts and actions on a daily basis. When you make purposeful decisions based on greater principles, others will respect you and you will feel better about yourself. When you stand on a foundation of meaning that is bigger than you, you will have a sense of self that is built from more than your talents, strengths, and experiences.

Many people get principles about 90 percent right, yet stay locked up and never achieve their goals because they miss an important detail or concept and refuse to change. They allow things like pride, emotions, education, comfort, and even interpretation of religious doctrine to keep from being effective in the pursuit of their goals. To avoid this stagnation, and years of possible misery, simply evaluate the results you are getting or not getting in life to determine whether you are effectively applying principles. Moving past 90 percent thinking requires an ongoing pursuit of growth and a willingness to change. God is the masterful teacher who is looking for humble and hungry students. Embrace and follow God's laws for the purpose they were intended—providing you the keys to unlock your fullest potential in life.

I want to hear from you. If you have questions, comments, or would like information regarding speaking availability contact me at:

Dr. Todd Bennett
1755 Westgate Drive
Suite 260
Boise, ID 83704

(208) 373-0790

Email: DrTodd@CornerstonePsy.com

You can also reach me through my website:
www.DrToddBennett.com

This website includes videos produced through www.IQuestions.com.